Let's Pray

James P Dumont

Pamela A Dumont

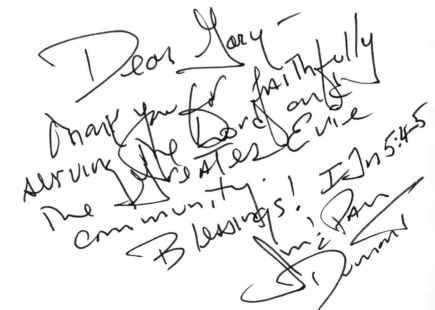

Dear Mary —
Thank you for faithfully
serving the Lord and
the ____ates Evie
community! Jn 5:45
Blessings! Jim & Pam
Dumont

Unless otherwise noted, all Scripture taken from the New King James Version®. Copyright © 1982 by Thomas Nelson. Used by permission. All rights reserved.

Scripture taken from the New Century Version®. Copyright © 2005 by Thomas Nelson. Used by permission. All rights reserved.

The Holy Bible: The Amplified Bible. 1987. 2015. La Habra, CA: The Lockman Foundation.

Holy Bible: New Living Translation. 1994, 2004, 2007, 2013. Carol Stream, IL: Tyndale House Publishers.

Holy Bible: Young's Literal Translation (YLT) Robert Young, Covenant Press.

Cover photo provided by Dr. Anna M. Dumont

DEDICATION

This book is lovingly dedicated to "The Power Team", our four grandkids, Jazna, Coleben, Symeon and Kendru. *"Here am I and the children whom the LORD has given me! We are for signs and wonders in Israel from the LORD of hosts, Who dwells in Mount Zion"* - Isaiah 8:18.

It is my great honor to recommend Jim and Pam Dumont's book, *"Let's Pray"*. I remember answering my phone and hearing the words, *"Pray for Jim Dumont. We don't know exactly what happened, but he is on the side of the road in Maine and they are performing CPR on him and it doesn't look good."* This book is a road map of what to do when your world collapses right before your eyes. This is the story of the faithfulness of God and how Pam, along with her family and church believed God for the impossible. It will not only inspire you, but help you prepare for the day when life may hand you an impossible situation. I tell you this, when "impossible" comes my way, you can be assured that I'm calling my friends, Jim and Pam and saying, "Let's Pray"!

Pastor John Nuzzo
Victory Family Church, Cranberry Twp., PA, USA

We have known Jim and Pam Dumont for over 15 years. We serve alongside them in overseeing and ministering to pastors and leaders in the northeast region of the United States.

Our lives have been greatly impacted by their deep devotion to God and His calling in their lives. They demonstrate in their lives the content they share in this book. Their love for people is very deep and visible. Their heart is to see people experience a relationship and life with Jesus Christ.

In their obedience to God to pioneer Erie Christian Fellowship and to faithfully served ECF as Senior Pastors for almost 30 years, we have seen them live out their convictions. As a result of their dedication to living a life of prayer, much has been accomplished and many lives have been changed for the Kingdom of God. "Let's Pray" is a lifestyle and a joy for them - not an obligation. This book will stir you to deepen your prayer life with your Heavenly Father.

Founding Pastor Sam & Sherlyn Smucker
Worship Center, Lancaster, PA, USA

ACKNOWLEDGMENTS

Our life has been a journey that would have been impossible without the support of both of our families.   Our families of origin as well as the spiritual families God brought into our lives gave us the courage and encouragement to continue.   Finally, our church family was there for us in our darkest hour.   Through them, Jesus fulfilled his promise in Matthew 28:20, "... **and lo, I am with you always, even to the end of the age.**"

CONTENTS

	Prologue	Pg. 1
Ch 1	Things About to Change	Pg. 3
Ch 2	Our Green House	Pg. 12
Ch 3	Prayer Opens Doors	Pg. 22
Ch 4	Pursuing God's Call	Pg. 30
Ch 5	From Tulsa to Texas	Pg. 34
Ch 6	Planted in Erie	Pg. 43
Ch 7	Building a Great Church	Pg. 54
Ch 8	Fresh Paint and Men in Black	Pg. 61
Ch 9	Beyond Our Four Walls	Pg. 68
Ch 10	Prayer and Unexpected Blessings	Pg. 75
Ch 11	An Architect Meets Jesus	Pg. 80
Ch 12	Deliverance and New Destiny	Pg. 86
Ch 13	A Praying Church - Pam	Pg. 91
Ch 14	At Death's Door - Pam	Pg. 98
Ch 15	The Long Week – Pam	Pg. 105
	Epilogue	Pg. 115

PROLOGUE

It was a beautiful September afternoon. To be exact, September 24, 2018. I had gone outside for a walk on the paved road beside Wilson Pond in North Monmouth, Maine. I only know these details because they were recounted to me. My life was about to change dramatically. It would be another week before I would hear the story.

We had driven 700 miles from Erie, Pennsylvania to Maine to care for my parents. They were both 92 years old and still living at home. Mom struggled with Alzheimer's dementia and dad was slowing down. My brother John and his wife Lisa lovingly provided ongoing care for the parents. Pam and I planned to give them a well-deserved break. They had already left for a week of wilderness camping in upstate Maine. We were watching the parents.

It was 4:30 pm and Pam was at the stove preparing the evening meal. Together, after 37 years of pastoral ministry, we had learned to hear and obey the inner promptings of the Holy Spirit.

Suddenly and unexpectantly, Pam had an urgent sense that something was terribly wrong. There was no verbal instruction but a clear and deep inner knowing that she must leave immediately and find me. Her head told her the foolishness and danger of leaving the unattended food on the stove. But through the practice of prayer, her heart had been trained to listen and to obey the Holy Spirit's promptings.

Darting out the door, she ran to the end of the driveway. As Pam overviewed the landscape, she could see a police car and two ambulances down the road by the public boat launch. A group of people were standing around someone lying in the middle of the road. Paramedics were working on that person desperately trying to get a heartbeat. Pam thought to herself, "That must be where Jim is. He's down there praying for someone who's been hurt."

Making her way towards the ambulances, Pam could see the person on the ground had a large belly and she immediately thought, "That's not Jim because he's very trim." But as she neared the activity, she could see the jogging pants of the person on the ground. Those were my pants. As the paramedics worked and she pressed through the crowd, she eventually saw the glassy and fixed eyes. They were yellow and red and lifeless. Only then did she recognize the familiar face and was shocked to know . . . it was Jim! It was me.

During CPR, air had filled my stomach making me look large and overweight. That's why Pam did not immediately recognize me. But thank God she had come. No one knew the person lying lifeless on the ground. I carried no identification. I was an out of town stranger walking by the lake.

God had prompted Pam to come looking for me. Our world was about to change. Prayer had already changed our lives in major ways. And now, our life would change again. Come with us as we go back in time and tell you the miracle of how it all happened for us. Prayer changed our lives and God promises to do the same for you! He desires to make Himself known and real to you. One of His great promises is found in Jeremiah 33:3, "Call to Me, and I will answer you, and show you great and mighty things, which you do not know." For me and Pam, it all began with the simple words, "Let's pray".

He meant for us to see Him, to live with Him, and to draw life from His Smile.

A.W. Tozer

Chapter 1
THINGS ABOUT TO CHANGE

Let's pray!

Little did I realize the life changing power behind that simple invitation. It was 1974 and I was a student at the University of Maine studying geology. I had just completed a 4-year enlistment in the U.S. Coast Guard serving as a Marine Science Technician Scuba Diver. As a college freshman, I was studying what I now humorously call "evolution and pollution". My professors talked about the long evolutionary history of the earth and man's gradual progression from primal slime to primate. God fit nowhere into this equation.

I was also taking courses highlighting man's environmental impact on the earth. To show his solidarity with "Mother Earth", one of my 40 something-year-old professors was still proudly wearing shirts from his high school years! This was his way to lessen the negative impact caused by the new synthetic fibers.

From what I was learning, things looked bleak down here on planet earth. Even though I grew up in a Roman Catholic family and served as the youngest altar boy at St. Patrick's Church in Lewiston, Maine, my faith had long ago vaporized. Four years in the Coast Guard had molded me into a "salty sailor". My thinking and behavior were now aligned with my training with the SEALS as a Navy diver and of a guy who spent 4 years on a ship cruising the Caribbean and North Atlantic.

Resolved at this point that God did not exist, I had no eternal hope and saw life as meaningless. Likely, this was Solomon's mindset towards the end of his life when he had lost his way and wrote, *"Everything is meaningless,"* says the Teacher, *"completely meaningless!"* - Ecclesiastes 1:2, NLT.

Having recently broken up with my college girlfriend, it looked like I was going to be alone on New Year's Eve 1974-75. Lou, the wife of my mobile home park neighbor would not let up until I agreed to attend the big party at their friend's place. They had invited some single ladies, so of course I agreed to go. Little did I know that I was about to meet the young woman who would become my bride and ministry life partner!

Pam was a cute little brunette employed at the Elizabeth Levinson Center in Bangor. She lovingly and tirelessly worked to care for severely handicapped children. She was excited to attend college in the coming year and to become an Occupational Therapist. We met and kissed at midnight. I know, it sounds like a fairytale, but it's true. That fall she left for Utica College in upstate New York and I remained at the University of Maine. We were now separated by 500 miles.

Back in Maine, Pam's dad was not so keen on me since I was by his definition, "a heathen". He was correct... I was. However, I thought I was a "good" heathen because I grew up in a Catholic family and was once an altar boy. By my self-assessment, I had accrued enough good deeds to compensate for any current infractions

While away at college, Pam was encouraged by her dad to attend a church called Love Inn. It might seem a little strange that out of concern for his daughter, he would encourage her to attend a place called, "Love Inn". To appreciate the name, you would have to understand the "flower child" culture of the late 60's that spilled over into the early 70's.

Love Inn was a "hippie type" church that blossomed out of the "Jesus Movement". These were college kids disillusioned by the Viet Nam conflict and tired of both the establishment and the "religious system". They were hungry and searching for a genuine spiritual reality.

Love Inn located just outside of Ithaca, New York was near Cornell University. The "church" met in a refurbished barn. The leader was Scott Ross, a "born again" radio DJ who had rubbed shoulders with many of the secular music artist of the time including the Beetles.

Somehow, way up in costal Maine, Pam's dad, John had picked up Love Inn's syndicated radio program! He wrote to Pam, sent her gas money and urged her to drive the two- and one-half hours to attend one of their services. I suppose he thought the spiritual influence would impact Pam and perhaps awaken her to flee from that heathen (me) pursuing his daughter.

One of the other leaders at Love Inn was Phil Keaggy, a celebrated guitarist and singer to this present day. Phil led worship. Together, Scott and Phil, with their amazing gifts but most importantly in their passion to reach a searching generation created an environment where young people were coming to Jesus and finding a genuine faith.

It was there that Pam found fresh fire for her faith. During one of the services, she was powerfully drawn to the front where she recommitted her life to Christ. Phil Keaggy laid hands on her (a Bible practice) and she was filled with the Holy Spirit. Life was about to change!

Pam and I communicated by phone once or twice each week, but conversations were always short. These were the days before cell phones. Making a long-distance call from Maine to New York always cost more than we could afford. I was scantily living on my $270 per month G.I. Bill. From that and savings, I paid my university tuition, rent, utilities and automobile expense. There was no financial breathing room.

On top of that, I would send Pam a few dollars whenever possible. I had a deep compassion for her because she was flat broke. Shampoo or a candy bar were special treats. Grants and personal loans made it possible for her to attend Utica College, but she had no financial assistance from home. Although her parents loved her, the modest military retirement her dad received rendered it impossible for the family to contribute to Pam's education.

One of the things that attracted me to Pam was her incredible work ethic and resolve to push through obstacles. When I first met her, she was living on the coast of Maine in a barn that she and her father converted into a unique home. Pam's dad had three daughters and no sons. I often joke that Pam was his only son in that she liked construction. Pam had a "get-er-done" spirit about her.

Along with Pam's help, Pam's dad had disassembled and transported their barn 125 miles from Danforth to South Penobscot, Maine. They had installed beautiful stained-glass windows acquired from abandoned churches. The living room window was made of two semicircle windows joined making a spectacular six-foot diameter stained window. It was amazing! On top of that, they had constructed a massive stone fireplace that swallowed huge logs. This was a unique home indeed!

Pam was never afraid to work! Before going away to college, she daily walked a mile through the woods up the dirt road to her car. She would then drive an hour into Bangor where she worked at the Elizabeth Levinson Center as an aid assisting severely handicapped children. It was there she learned about Occupational Therapy and one of the few colleges at the time offering this major, Utica College in upstate New York. That's how she landed in Utica.

About a week after Pam's spiritual encounter at Love Inn, I called her on the phone and the conversation went something like this.

"Hi Pam, how are you!"

"Hi sweetie, I'm doing great!"

"What have you been up to?"

"Oh. . . school and I drove out to Ithaca last weekend to visit the place my father has been writing me about...you know, Love Inn. He sent gas money for me to get there."

"That's great. What else is new?"

"Well...while I was there, I had an amazing experience...and, I recommitted my life to Jesus."

Dead silence on my end.

Thoughts immediately flooded my mind. What does this mean? How is this going to affect our relationship? How can she let Jesus into her life without checking with me? I'm the man in her life, not Jesus!

I am not proud of it, but that was my mindset at the time. Remember, I was a "heathen". I was confused and determined to get answers. I loved Pam but at the same time I was afraid or unwilling to make a serious commitment to her while in this long-distance relationship. My heart and head were in serious conflict, but one thing for sure. . . I was committed to rescuing Pam from the religious fanatics. So, after hanging up, I resolved to get to the bottom of things!

Pam's dad had recently given me a copy of, "The Late Great Planet Earth" by Hal Lindsey. I'm sure he did so in hopes of spiritually reaching me. After reading the book, I remember thinking, "Is it possible there is life beyond our time on this earth?" The idea seemed surreal, yet it stirred hope, curiosity and anticipation in my heart.

The Bible says, "The entrance of Your words gives light; It gives understanding to the simple" - Psalm 119:130. The message of that book stood in stark contrast to the idea of simply being an evolved primate. It brought hope to me. Was it possible that life continued beyond the grave? Was it possible that when you died, you were not dead like a dog?

So, in my quest to rescue Pam and "find the truth", I did something I had not done for years. I prayed. My honest to goodness prayer went something like this: "God if you really exist, please help me by providing financial assistance so I can drive to Utica and save Pam from the religious fanatics or find out if this is real." The next day I went to the

University bulletin board and immediately located a couple wanting a ride to Utica, New York on the same dates I was planning to go! Wow...had God already answered my prayer?

After connecting with the couple, we left Orono, Maine for Utica, New York on Good Friday afternoon, April 16, 1976. Little did I realize what was in store for me on this journey!

Arriving at the Utica campus, I found Pam's dorm. Most of the students were gone for the long Easter weekend so it looked like there would be no problem with me staying in the girl's dorm over the weekend. I was excited and apprehensive to meet Pam. Had she changed? Would she be different now that she was a "holy woman"? At least, that's how I now viewed Pam having rededicated her life to Jesus. These were the thoughts racing through my mind as I stood outside her dorm room and knocked on the door.

Soon the door swung open and Pam and I stood face to face, not sure what to do. Should I hug her or shake her hand? How does one greet a "holy woman"? I was not sure of the proper protocol, but I quickly found the courage to embrace her. It was wonderful to be together again.

We were soon in her room talking about school but mostly about the recent big changes in her spiritual life. I was brimming with questions. What does this all mean? Is it real? Can anyone have the same experience? What does it mean to receive Jesus? What does this mean for us? My questions popped quicker than she could answer. Finally, Pam said, "Let's pray".

Kneeling by her bed on the floor, I tried recalling the "Our Father" or some other prayer from my altar boy days. Instead, I began to hear Pam praying in the most beautiful language imaginable. It was beautiful but at the same time it scared me. I knew this was supernatural. I knew Pam was not studying a language and even if she was, she would not be this fluent already. I was keenly aware something supernatural was happening.

The Bible speaks of the gift of the Holy Spirit accompanied with the gift of "tongues" or a God given supernatural prayer language. Pam had received that wonderful gift. It is the ability to pray in a God given language that flows from one's spirit rather than the mind (Acts 2:4). I was unprepared for such a quick introduction to Biblical Christianity, so I asked Pam to please stop. I needed time to process. Whoa. . .this trip was turning into more than I expected! Later that evening we went out to grab something to eat and to talk.

The next morning, we hit the books. Pam's roommate was gone for the weekend, so Pam and I sat on opposite ends of the room studying. My mind would drift in and out of my coursework as I tried to make sense of what had happened the previous evening. Gradually, thoughts of my studies took a back seat as troubling thoughts captivated my mind. I know now how the devil operates because he was laying it on thick that day. Thoughts such as, "You had better get out of here. Pam has gone nuts and you will too if you don't leave now."

This went on for a few minutes until Pam looked over and saw my troubled state. "What's wrong, honey", she gently asked? "Pam, I don't understand what is happening." Before I could say another word, Pam jumped in with what was becoming her standard response, "Let's pray!"

This time, I sat on the bed and Pam knelt on the floor. Innocently, Pam began to pray in her new "prayer language" as I began pouring out my heart in desperation to God. All I could say were the words I found spilling out of my heart, "God, I have got to know You...God, I have got to know You., God, I have got to know You!" I'm not sure how long I repeated this plea, but God was about to reveal Himself to me big time!

Suddenly, I had a profound awareness that I was hopelessly lost. I lay spiritually naked before a Holy God. I was aware in very specific detail of my many sins and transgressions. I knew in a general sense that I was spiritually lost and in a very profound sense I knew that I was responsible for my separation from God. All I could do was weep in anguish and sorrow for my rebellion and pride. An unpassable chasm separated me from a Holy God. Although I was totally unfamiliar with the Bible, I had a deep sense of the meaning of God's words in Isaiah 59:2; "But your iniquities have separated you from your God; And your sins have hidden His face from you, so that He will not hear."

In my agony and distress, I soon rolled off the bed and now lay flat on the floor in a puddle of tears. Pam was concerned because I was literally wailing in anguish over my desperate spiritual state. What should she do? She kept telling me, "Jim, its ok, you just have to ask for forgiveness", but I heard none of it. God had stripped away my spiritual blinders, so I could view my true spiritual state. I was guilty, condemned and hopelessly lost!

In desperation, Pam pleaded, "Lord, what should I do?"

In that instant, Pam had a vision of a billboard. On the billboard was written the Bible verse, "Matthew 9:2". Pam had no idea what that verse said. Immediately, reaching for her Bible she found the passage and there in big red letters Jesus says, *"Take heart, my son; your sins are forgiven."* Joy and amazement filled her heart as she slid her Bible under my nose that was now pressed to the floor in a puddle of tears.

Jesus' words leaped off the page and into me like flashes of lightning. In an instant, my countenance changed from anguish and sorrow to jubilation. I was forgiven! Now my tears became tears of joy and gratitude. The emotion was impossible to contain as I continued to weep, but now in gratitude for the mercy and grace being poured into my life.

Pam was now becoming concerned that campus security, hearing all the emotion and tears, would come. So, once again, she turned to God and said, "What do I do now?" Again, she had a vision of a billboard. This time the verse on the billboard was Luke 7:13-14. Again, Jesus speaking in this passage says in big red letters, **"Do not weep. Young man I say**

unto you arise."

Having found the passage, Pam once again slid her Bible under my nose. Again, Jesus' words shot through my heart giving me the strength to rise to my feet. As I arose, God now graciously granted me a heavenly vision. I saw multitudes of people. It was like a sea of people. And, as I viewed this mass of humanity, it was as though someone pulled a dark curtain over them. And then the Lord spoke to my heart saying, "That is the fate of every person who does not know Jesus Christ as their personal Lord and Savior."

I do not remember leaving the room that day. I do remember driving to Love Inn in Ithaca the next day where I was water baptized in a farm pond on Easter Sunday, April 18th, 1976. They might have had to chip away ice from the pond that day, but I was adamant. I was going to be water baptized. I was a new man!

The purpose of prayer is that we a get a hold of God, not the answer. The answer is a bonus.

Oswald Chambers

Chapter 2
OUR GREEN HOUSE

My world would never again to be the same. The Bible says, "Therefore, if anyone is in Christ, he is a new creation; old things have passed away; behold, all things have become new" - II Corinthians 5:17. That was certainly my experience.

Back in Orono, Maine, I remember walking across the University concourse and looking up at the sky. Everything seemed to be in technicolor. The sky was bluer, the clouds whiter and puffier. It was like I was seeing the world through clear corrective lenses.

This experience continued for a few weeks until the day to day routine and pressures of school began kicking in. I had no Christian friends or church family to provide spiritual support and I needed a spiritual lift. Satan had once again begun to mess with my mind.

Every day I would drive past a McDonalds on my way to classes. I never stopped because it was a major luxury I could not afford. But, for some reason that day, I felt compelled to stop at least for a cup of coffee.

Sitting in the dining area sipping my coffee (and wondering why I was doing this since I was running late), I noticed three men walk into the restaurant and I immediately recognized two of them. One was an old high school acquaintance who dropped off the radar from those of us who used to drink and party together. The other was my 7th grade health teacher whom I had not seen for years. Seeing me sitting alone, they immediately joined me.

It had been over six years since I had seen Jerry, my high school friend. It was strange to see him now, far from our hometown. Instantly, I knew exactly what had happened to him. All of us who use to run together thought he had gone off the deep end. He had stopped drinking and carousing. The word had gone out that he had "became religious". Now, in seeing him, I knew exactly what had happened. He had received Jesus as his Savior and been "born again". He too, like me, had become a "new creation" in Christ (II Corinthians 5:17)!

What a fortuitous meeting God had ordained! Jerry and my former health teacher (now a Pastor) and their friend and ministry partner were on their way to Canada to share the gospel. They had felt compelled to exit the highway and stop at the McDonalds where I was sitting alone, needing spiritual encouragement. After they poured into my life that morning, I came away knowing that God had not forgotten me now that I was alone back in Maine. His Word declares, "...I will never leave you, nor forsake you" - Hebrews 13:5. My plea and prayer for help had been answered!

Meanwhile the 1976 academic year was winding to a close. Pam and I continued to communicate by phone planning next steps for our future. We knew we needed to be together, but how? Occupational Therapy was not a Major offered at the University of Maine, but Geology was offered at Syracuse University. Syracuse and Utica were 50 miles apart. What if we both moved to upstate New York and commuted to our respective schools?

If we were going to do this, we needed to be married. That was step number one. In our mind, we were determined and compelled to do things in a God honoring way. He had become the center of our life. How could we now leave Him out of our plans? That thought never crossed our minds.

So, to everyone's chagrin, we announced our wedding plans for May 29th, Labor Day weekend, 1976. Many of Pam's friends thought for sure she must be pregnant. Why else would we marry so quickly? But that was not the case. We were just making sure to do everything right. All we knew was that God had reached down and done a miracle in our lives and we were ready to move forward with His plans whatever they may be. For us, that meant we were to be together. Somehow, He would make a way.

After our May wedding and weekend honeymoon at Bar Harbor, I went to work for the Maine Department of Environmental Protection during the summer of 1976. I applied to Syracuse University and was immediately accepted. Now we just needed to trust God for living arrangements in the fall!

At this point, Pam and I were very young and childlike in our faith. Jesus' words in Mark 10:15 describes us quite well. "Assuredly, I say to you, whoever does not receive the kingdom of God as a little child will by no means enter it." Our childlikeness did not mean spiritual weakness. Rather, it meant we were quick to trust and obey God. We did not see obstacles. Rather, we only saw our amazing God. Nothing could stand in front of us if we followed hard after Him.

So, our plan was, in the fall, we would drive to upstate New York and find a town half way between Syracuse and Utica. There we would set up our home and travel to our respective colleges. No problem...except this did not make sense to my sister-in-law at the time.

Growing up in a totally irreligious environment, she thought Pam and I were naïve, bordering on crazy. She would rail on us for our decisions which did not make sense to her mind. It was never pleasant to be in her company.

One Sunday, my parents had hosted a dinner at their home. My sister-in-law was there and after the meal, she, Pam and my mother were at the kitchen sink washing dishes. My sister-in-law had already begun to lay into Pam. "You and Jim are just crazy with your ridiculous decisions. You are going to drive out to New York, and you don't even know where you are going! That's crazy!" This went on and on as I sat patiently at the kitchen table eavesdropping on their conversation.

As previously mentioned, Pam and I were taking the Bible, God's Word as our que. One Scripture in particular, Hebrews 11:8, greatly encouraged and strengthened our faith. "By faith Abraham obeyed when he was called to go out to the place which he would receive as an inheritance. And he went out, not knowing where he was going." We were confident that God would lead and guide us to the right place…the place He was preparing for us. After all, God is no respecter of persons. If He did this for Abraham, He would do it for us too!

That Sunday afternoon, as Pam continued to be pressed with questions she could not answer, she suddenly blurted out, "We are going to live in a green house. We have a green house!" Whaaat! My mind suddenly went tilt. Now I'm thinking . . . Pam what are you saying! Of course, my sister-in-law immediately jumped on this. "You are going to live in a green house. Is that right. How are you going to do that?"

I'm ashamed to admit it, but at this point I was quite embarrassed for me and Pam. I'm thinking to myself, you and Pam have already done enough stuff to cause everyone to think you are nuts. Now, Pam is making crazy statements that are impossible to fulfill.

This situation was not unlike when God told Abraham and Sarah that they would have a child in their old age and Sarah laughed at the impossibility of it. God's response was, "Is anything too hard for the Lord?" - Genesis 18:11-14.

I did not realize the responsibility to deliver on God's promise did not rest upon me and Pam. God had spoken through Pam's mouth and He would deliver on the promise. Regardless, we left my parent's house that day feeling foolish and embarrassed. Pam and I needed to talk!

When we were alone, Pam explained what had happened. As she stood at the sink under the unyielding scrutiny and inquisition, suddenly, she had seen a two-story green house with a quaint front porch and a large maple tree. The picture was as clear as day. It was not unlike the experience where, at my conversion, she had seen the billboards. So, she had simply spoken what she had seen. The ongoing provocations drove away all fears and Pam had boldly stepped out to proclaim what God had shown her.

Pam had a proven track record I could never deny. My powerful conversion experience was still fresh in my heart and mind. How could I doubt Pam's word? Nevertheless, we would have to walk through this experience and see how God would fulfill His promise.

Summer ended, and the time came for us to begin our journey to school. We stuffed my 1973 Saab 96 and Pam's 1970 AMC Hornet with our belongings, said goodbye to family, and headed off to travel the 400 miles to upstate New York. On our road map we had located Canastota, New York, a small-town midway between Syracuse and Utica just off Route 5. That was our destination.

Arriving in Canastota later in the day, I remember we found a place on the grassy city square on Route 5 where we knelt and prayed. "God, you have led us here, now please direct our steps. In Jesus name. Amen!" The next thing we did was find a small one room boarding house where we could stay the night. It was simple, but inexpensive.

The next morning, we began our search. We drove through neighborhoods and whenever we would see a green colored house with a "for sale" sign, Pam would get excited and say, "Stop, there's one!". In frustration I would remind her, "Honey, we're living on my G.I. Bill which is only $270 per month. We have no money to purchase a home and just barely enough to get into a rent."

After a day or two of searching, I finally convinced Pam it was time to get some assistance. So, we found a real estate agent and told him we were looking for housing. He told us he knew of two school teachers who purchased and renovated homes during the summer months. In fact, right now they were working on a home. He would get in touch with them and find out if anything was available.

I remember the agent then telling us, "Let me handle this. Why don't you take a ride and visit the New Your State Fair in Syracuse?" That sure sounded good, but that's not where our focus was at the time. We were living out of two cars and trying to hold on to whatever cash we had. Who knew what expenses were before us?

A day later the agent returned and told us he had connected with the teachers. In fact, the teachers were only a week away from finishing an apartment in a home they had been working on throughout the summer. They had divided the two-story home into three apartments. The unit near completion was a one-bedroom unit. We negotiated a lower price and made plans to move in the following week.

But . . . there was only one big problem. The house was white. How would we explain this to the folks back home considering Pam's proclamation, "We have a green house?" We never said a word to the agent or teachers regarding our home color choice. Our major concern was moving out of our cars and into someplace with a roof over our heads, so we could prepare for school.

Anxious to unload our vehicles, the teachers graciously gave us permission to start moving things to the apartment before our official move in date. So, one afternoon, we pulled up to the front of the house. There were the two teachers, working. One was standing on scaffolding painting and the second, seeing our car, immediately came running our way. He was profusely apologetic and kept saying, "I'm so sorry, I'm so sorry. Please let me explain."

Before we could say a word, he began gushing out his story. "Me and my partner were going to paint this house brown. We went to the paint store to purchase brown paint and for some reason we came home with green paint." Sure enough, we could see a six-foot square green section of the house. They had already started painting the house a beautiful deep forest green...exactly the color Pam had seen in her vision!

He went on, "We are so sorry. We can't stand this green color, but you are the ones who will live here. What do you think?" Pam and I stared at each other with eyes like saucers and then immediately consoled our new landlord by assuring him WE LOVED their color choice! All the while, we were jumping up and down on our insides, awed by the miracle God had performed in response to our childlike faith and prayer.

When word of our green home arrived back to our family in Maine, my sister in law would have believed us if we told her cows in upstate New York gave chocolate milk. Our credibility suddenly went through the ceiling. God had heard our prayer and proved Himself to be faithful!

After moving into our apartment, we gradually settled into the new academic year. Being a morning person, I would daily arise, make coffee and lovingly coach Pam out of bed. We were both exhausted from late study nights but very happy. After a quick breakfast, Pam would be on the road driving east towards Utica and I would head west towards Syracuse. The two cities were 50 miles apart.

Soon, we found a new start up church in East Syracuse, Christian Church of the Resurrection. The church was led by a wonderful Lebanese man, Pastor Saied Adore and his wife Esther. Although the church was small in numbers, the people were passionate for Jesus. These were our kind of people! It was perfect for us.

The church demographics beautifully exemplified how Jesus' love creates a common bond among people from all walks of life. Both professionals and simple folk attended. I remember the warmth we felt both at church and in attending home groups hosted in various homes.

In the church was another young couple that ministered to us. Chad, the husband had a definite prophetic gift. New Testament prophecy is more forthtelling (speaking forth inspired words of encouragement) than foretelling (telling the future). In other words, New Testament prophecy is primarily for edification, exhortation and comfort and not necessarily telling the future.

One evening, Chad had a prophetic word for me that did have an element of foretelling the future. He and his wife had invited us to dinner at their home. Later in the evening as we were preparing to leave, Chad took me aside and began to speak the words God had placed in his heart. "God", he said, "shows me a solid pillar. You are that pillar. You will be a pillar in His church."

Those words took me back. Wow...what was God saying? My powerful conversion experience was still very real, but I was studying to become a geologist. Nevertheless, I did as Mary, Jesus' mother when prophetic words were given to her: She "... kept all these things and pondered them in her heart" - Luke 2:19.

And that's exactly what I did. I put those words "on a shelf" in my heart. Later the time would come when God would fulfill His plans and purposes for me and Pam. Like the green house incident, it was not our responsibility to make things happen. Our responsibility was to stay spiritually hungry and to follow close after Jesus.

What played a big part in my initially coming to faith was when I had been powerfully introduced to the Holy Spirit in Pam's dorm room. At the time of my conversion, that experience had convinced me of the reality of the supernatural. It set me up to understand that God and the Bible were real. The result was I had yielded my life to Jesus.

Since that time, I had come to understand that the gift of the Holy Spirit was a promise given to every born-again believer. In Acts 2:38-39, Peter declares, "Repent, and let every one of you be baptized in the name of Jesus Christ for the remission of sins; and you shall receive the gift of the Holy Spirit. For the promise is to you and to your children, and to all who are afar off, as many as the Lord our God will call."

At home I would hear Pam pray in her prayer language and then at church I would hear other believers doing the same. I wanted that gift so bad, but I was trying to receive with my head instead of with my heart. This is exactly where we often miss it when it comes to receiving anything from God.

Romans 10:9–10 says, "That if you confess with your mouth the Lord

Jesus and *believe in your heart* that God has raised Him from the dead, you will be saved. For *with the heart* one believes unto righteousness, and with the mouth confession is made unto salvation."

If you look closely at this scripture, you will note that two times it speaks of believing with your heart. Your heart is your spirit. Often the problem is we try to believe with our head and not with our heart. That was my problem.

I would read God's promises about the Holy Spirit and get excited to receive. But my head would tell me, "Yes, the baptism in the Holy Spirit is real, but it's not for you." That's exactly what the devil wanted me to believe. I never seemed to get beyond that point, and I would give up. By nature, and being a guy, I was more cerebral in my approach to things and especially so since I was training in the sciences.

But on Easter Sunday, 1977 things were about to change. We had gone to church and enjoyed a wonderful Spirit filled service. I had come away disappointed that I had yet to receive the gift of the Holy Spirit accompanied with a personal prayer language. I continually thought about it on the 35-minute drive home. As we returned to our apartment in Canastota, a resolve took hold of my heart.

Opposite our second-floor apartment was another apartment being renovated by our landlords. The apartment was unlocked and vacant. I told Pam, please hold lunch because I'm going into that apartment and I'm not coming out until I am baptized in the Holy Spirit and receive my prayer language. I was determined to stay there all day if necessary!

Sometimes it takes that kind of resolve to receive from God. Throughout the Bible we find instances of people whose determination to receive would not be denied. Hebrews Chapter 11 is filled with stories of people with that kind of faith. God delights in them.

I walked into that small unfinished apartment and headed to a corner where I immediately knelt to pray. I remember saying, "Father, I'm in here today to receive. Your Word says to ask, and you shall receive. I don't understand everything about the Holy Spirit. I just know I want to receive the gift of the Holy Spirit according to Your Word. Now I've asked and asked, and I'm frustrated from asking. Now, I'm just going to thank You because Mark 11:23-24 says when you pray to believe you receive. So now, I'm thanking You for the gift of the Holy Spirit in Jesus' Name. Amen!"

I then lifted my hands and began to thank God for the gift of the Holy Spirit. I did that for about 30 seconds and before I knew it, I had slipped over into a heavenly language. I was baptized in the Holy Spirit. Then I began to shout!

The following February we experienced a delightful surprise. Pam was pregnant! Our plans were changing but it was because God was giving us the greatest blessing we could ever imagine! Immeasurably more valuable than the careers we were chasing was the little boy in Pam's womb. One day he would grow up and become a Medical doctor. In fact, one day he would save my life from a choking episode and years later play a key part in my recovery from a death to life experience. When May came around, we headed back to Maine!

No praying man or woman accomplishes so much with so little expenditure of time as when he or she is praying.

C.E. Cowman

Chapter 3
PRAYER OPENS DOORS

Moving back to Maine, my parents graciously allowed us to transform their garage into a temporary summer suite. There, we draped decorative sheets and blankets on the walls, gathered some makeshift furniture and camped out. That summer, I was again employed by the Maine Department of Environmental Protection, Lakes Division.

Years prior to this, when I was about 14 or 15 years old, I had gained some notoriety stirring environmental awareness in Maine. My brother along with my friend Rick and I had acquired and restored a beat up, 12-foot flat bottom boat. With an old outboard engine, every fall we traversed Sabattus lake from my grandparent's home to Dead River to hunt ducks.

I was always aware of the environmental quality of the lake as every year the water became soupy green because of algae blooming. I noted that a major egg producer annually dumped tons of raw chicken manure on the banks of the Dead River. This adversely upset the entire lake ecosystem and greatly concerned me.

So, as a 15-year-old, I took a water sample and sent it with a letter to the Maine Department of Environmental Protection in Augusta. Their response was to thank me for my concern and to tell me they had no ability to analyze water samples.

So, I wrote a letter to the editor of the Lewiston Sun Journal newspaper. It resulted in people assembling in protest on the banks of the Dead River and hanging an 8-foot plywood chicken "in effigy". The whole assembly and protest were aired by the local news!

Fast forward to the summer of 1977 and my current summer job at the Maine DEP Lakes Division. One afternoon strolling into the office my supervisor tossed a folder on my desk. Smiling, he quipped, "Hey Dumont, check this out". Inside was historic information on lake Sabattus, including the newspaper clipping of my letter to the editor dating back to 1966! My passion for lake preservation preceded his tenure at the DEP.

As summer ended, Pam and I headed north to Orono where I would complete my senior year at the University of Maine. Justin, our joy was born in November and soon May and graduation time arrived. What would we do next?

I greatly struggled with pursuing a career in my field of training. God had supernaturally called us to ministry, but we had no idea how to pursue that call. I loved environmental studies and it seemed that door was opening for me. At the same time, it was impossible to shake the awareness that there was something immeasurably more valuable to be preserved; the precious souls of men and women. The Bible says, "For what will it profit a man if he gains the whole world, and loses his own soul?" - Mark 8:36.

It is important to note that a "call to ministry" is a supernatural call. It is not something a person chooses for oneself. Rather, it is a compelling urge to lead, to preach and to impact people's lives. It is something that God supernaturally imparts into the heart of the one He calls. The Bible says in Hebrews 5:4, "And no man takes this honor to himself, but he who is called by God, just as Aaron was."

As an illustration, I remember taking a speech class my senior year at university. In my class was a young man who told me when he graduated, he planned to attend seminary. His father, a denominational minister, had told him that the ministry was a good profession. He had convinced his son to pursue a ministry "career". The way was smoothly paved for this young man. His father had connections and it would be a natural transition for him to go from University to Seminary.

Soon the time came for him to give his speech. He arose and gave a boring talk about how wrong it was for people to smoke in public places. Sitting there listening to him, I was unable to reconcile in my mind how someone so privileged to enter ministry could speak of nothing more important than smoking in public places!

Likely, this young man did not possess God's divine call upon his life. For whatever reasons, his father had convinced him to enter seminary, but it appeared God had not. I truly felt sorry for this young man because ministry is a high and demanding call.

There are supernatural gifts and impartations that accompany a genuine call to ministry. How sad to intrude into an office for which one is ill prepared and unequipped. I thought of the many people who, listening to this young man, would be influenced to think that the gospel was nothing more than a charge to become a socially conscious person.

When I gave my speech, I spoke to the class on C.S. Lewis' premise that Jesus was either liar, a lunatic or Lord. According to Lewis, Jesus' bold statements, taken at face value, necessitate that He fall into one of those categories. After examining the evidence, we must make a critical choice. Jesus is Lord! And, "whoever calls on the name of the Lord shall be saved" - Romans 10:13.

For me and Pam the critical time had finally arrived. What would be our next steps after graduation? By now, we had learned the power of prayer. I couldn't shake the memories of the many times Pam had whispered, "Let's Pray". Proverbs 19:21 says, "There are many plans in a man's heart, nevertheless the Lord's counsel—that will stand." We determined that we would get the Lord's council before we took further steps!

So, one weekend in May 1978, Pam took our son Justin and went to the coast to visit her parents. I stayed alone in Orono at our university apartment. I had learned that fasting and prayer was a way of pressing closer to God. Fasting did not "persuade God to move". Rather, it caused one to become more sensitive to His promptings.

I believe fasting and prayer also demonstrate our sincere hunger for the things that are greater than food and water. The Bible says, "But without faith it is impossible to please Him, for he who comes to God must believe that He is, and that He is a rewarder of those who diligently seek Him" -Hebrews 11:6. We were hungry to know and receive God's plans and purposes!

Beginning my weekend fast I prayed, "Lord, we need your wisdom and direction. We are at crossroads and don't know which way to go. I'm fasting to know your will. You know my heart hungers to serve you in ministry, but we have no money and I'm graduating with a family. Thank you for showing us the way. In Jesus Name, Amen."

Immediately following that weekend fast, the Bangor Daily News published a solicitation for a Water Quality Planner in Aroostook County, Maine. After submitting my resume', I was invited to drive the two and one-half hours north for an interview. I will never forget that meeting.

The interview was at the Northern Maine Regional Planning Commission in Caribou. The Planning Commission was a quasi-governmental entity that Mr. B had single handedly organized and built through astute business and political connections. I was scheduled to meet personally with Mr. B.

When I arrived, I found the Commission was housed in an expansive old mansion repurposed and converted into a hub of activity. Working there were planners, engineers and support staff. Mr. B's office was massive. The day of my interview, I entered and there he sat, swallowed in a leather chair behind a massive mahogany desk. Walking into his office, you knew you had entered the Presidential suite!

Sitting opposite Mr. B, I felt like George Bailey sitting opposite Mr. Potter in the movie, "It's a Wonderful Life.". In many ways Mr. B was like Mr. Potter, having his hands in everything happening in Aroostook County. But the thing I remember most about that day was Mr. B's first words to me when he finally looked up from his desk. Fixing his eyes on me with a somewhat puzzled look on his face he said, "I've seen you sitting in that chair". "I don't understand this", he continued, "but I feel like I have met you before." In that instance, I knew God was working on our behalf!

As the interview wound down, Mr. B looked me straight in the eye and said, "I was going to hire someone else for this job, but I'm going to hire you." On his face was the same puzzled expression we had seen on the faces of the teachers who painted our green house in Canastota, New York. I could not wait to get to a phone and tell Pam! God had heard our prayer!

Aroostook County soon became our new home. After moving there, we learned that the region's major resource was open fields with rocky soil that produced excellent potatoes. The climate was well suited for potato production with short summers and long cold winters.

We moved into a temporary apartment in Caribou but soon leased an airy old home with a barn in the town of Washburn. My father once tactfully commented after a visit, "This is a nice place to be from". The critical word being, "from".

As always, Pam and I looked for a church where we could fellowship with other believers and continue our spiritual growth. We soon found a church family and became fast friends with the administrator of the church's school, John Toomer and his wife, Jeanne.

John soon became a spiritual mentor to me. Once a week he and I would meet for breakfast, Bible study and prayer at his home in Fort

Fairfield. The 21-mile, 5 AM drive on freezing winter mornings was worth the inconvenience for the spiritual support and encouragement I received. John had been introduced to Kenneth Copeland Ministries and soon he was sharing with me the things he had learned.

For instance, John and Jeanne were once visiting at our home. Justin, our son was just a toddler and like all toddlers, he loved to explore the lower cupboards and rearrange the pots and pans. Lovingly, but in ignorance, whenever Justin entered the kitchen we would say, "Here comes trouble"!

Immediately picking up on this, John began to teach us what the Bible says about the power of our words. Proverbs 18:21 says, "Death and life are in the power of the tongue, and those who love it will eat its fruit." We had previously experienced the positive power of words in our green house experience. John was showing us the Biblical truth that words play a big part in setting the course of our life.

As soon as we became aware of the power of our words, we quickly changed our vocabulary. Instead of saying, "Here comes trouble", when Justin entered the room we began to say, "Here comes a blessing"! Thank God, our son and his wife Anna have grown to become a great blessing to us and to many through their medical practices.

Each week John would loan me a fresh Kenneth Copeland teaching cassette. I had purchased a "portable" but bulky cassette player and strapped it to my belt. While traveling or at home, I would listen to the message again and again until the Word of God took root in my heart.

I highly treasured each cassette tape in this pre-internet era of 1978. The Bible says, "So then faith comes by hearing, and hearing by the word of God" (Rom 10:17). My faith and understanding were growing. Pam and I had many faith experiences with God, but we desperately needed solid Bible teaching. John had introduced us to this through the teachings of Kenneth Copeland.

One day John shocked me when, during our meeting time, he told me that Kenneth Copeland had a mentor by the name of Kenneth E. Hagin. I remember thinking, "Is it possible that anyone knows spiritually more than Kenneth Copeland!" In fact, John said, Kenneth E. Hagin had opened a Bible School in Tulsa, Oklahoma. At that instance, I knew this was a door to be explored. Was this, in fact, the open door to ministry that we had long been seeking?

My employment at the Planning Commission was going well, but in my heart of heart I could not shake the call of God upon my life. During my tenure at the Commission, I worked to identify and find solutions to the major cause of water pollution in Aroostook County - agricultural runoff of chemicals. I submitted for funding a test case to identify and quantify the problem.

Eventually the EPA funded this project and the results caused all manner of controversy because it quantified the magnitude of the problem of chemical agricultural runoff. It seemed like I was destined to stir controversy towards water preservation in the state of Maine. But God had other plans.

This was another moment when prayer was needed. I became convinced that we should apply to Kenneth E. Hagin's new school in Tulsa, Rhema Bible Training Center. Pam, on the other hand, was not so convinced. In fairness to Pam, it's important to understand her background.

Pam's entire childhood was spent moving every two years from California, to North Dakota to New Jersey to Massachusetts to England, etc., as her father was transferred because of his Air Force missile assignments during the cold war era. Pam was, in fact, born in Japan.

She had never settled in a home and we had never established roots since being married. Finally, we had somewhat settled. I had a job, an option to buy on our home and we had a toddler needing care. Now, I was suggesting another cross country move and then stepping into the unknowns of ministry!

For all that God has done in our lives, I must give Him all the glory. But, none of it would have been possible without the love, dedication and devotion of my Pam. When she and I were apart at our respective colleges and Pam had recommitted her life to Jesus at Love Inn, she was faced with the reality that I may not come to faith in Jesus.

Nevertheless, she had decided and prayed, "Even if I lose him, I will follow you, Jesus". For that decision, I will forever love and respect her. The only way to tap into a lifelong sustaining marital love is to first surrender to the love of Jesus. Then, our love for Jesus must supersede our love for any other person. "He who loves father or mother more than Me is not worthy of Me. And he who loves son or daughter more than Me is not worthy of Me" - Matt 10:37. Those are sobering words from Jesus.

This was a moment when the tables were turned. God had called me to put Him first. As much as I loved Pam, I could never shake my love for Jesus nor the call He had placed upon my life. I could never neglect the image of multitudes of lost people stepping into eternal darkness. I could never live with myself if I turned my back on what God had entrusted to me.

After seeking God in prayer, He had given me a scripture, Genesis 20:1, "And Abraham journeyed from there to the South. . ." We were living about as far north as you could go in the continental U.S., so I figured heading south to Tulsa was the right move. After conversation and much prayer, Pam was on board. We were moving to Tulsa!

Low expectations are the byproduct of prayerlessness, but prayer has a way of God-sizing our expectations.

Mark Batterson

Chapter 4
PURSUING GOD'S CALL

At the time, we were still driving our 1973 Saab 96. This "VW Bug" style vehicle would transport us and our belongs the 2000 miles to Tulsa. It was time to seriously downsize!

We gave our Pastor the new washer and dryer we had received for Christmas and sold the few furniture items we had acquired. Somehow, we carved out space in the back for Justin's car seat. We needed room for air to circulate because the Saab had no air conditioning and we were heading south.

The night before we left, friends helped install ball joints on the Saab. In the morning, we were ready to chase God's plans for our lives. We had lots of faith but barely enough cash to get to Tulsa and no credit cards to lean on. Frankly, it was best we had no credit cards because it forced us to place a demand on heaven's supply. Our plan was to make the trip in segments, camping along the way.

We were taking our que from 2 Corinthians 5:7, "For we walk by faith, not by sight". If we made our plans and decisions based on what we could see, we would never have stepped out into our destiny. Many people, moved only by what they see, fail to receive God's best for their lives. Jeremiah 29:11 says, "For I know the thoughts that I think toward you, says the Lord, thoughts of peace and not of evil, to give you a future and a hope."

We had no assurance of a place to stay in Tulsa except a lead given to us by our friends, Wayne and Marilyn Thibeau. The Thibeaus were seed potato growers in Aroostook County and members of Maranatha Assembly, the church we attended. One of their children was a student at Oral Roberts University in Tulsa. Months before, she had written home telling her parents about a posting she had seen at the ORU campus.

A Tulsa family was looking for a couple to assist with their young sons and to do some seasonal yard work. In exchange, a garage apartment was provided as well as a stipend of $200. per month. Unfortunately, before we left Maine, word got back that the position had been filled. We were, of course, disappointed but our confidence was that God would provide.

After a long trip, we arrived in Tulsa and camped out at the Will Rogers KOA campground in Claremore, OK. We were quick to notice that most people "camping out" were doing so in the convenience of travel trailers, RV's or Fifth Wheels with air conditioning units. We were the only ones in a tent and we soon discovered why!

July temperatures in Tulsa can hover in the mid 90's. The only reprieve we could find from the heat was by the campground pool. Soon after arriving, I was anxious to attend Kenneth Hagin's annual "Campmeeting" in downtown Tulsa. Pam though it wise for her to remain at the campground and let Justin enjoy the pool. So, one day I drove into Tulsa alone.

I returned in the late afternoon to find Pam desperate to escape the heat. The day had been intolerable. Camping in Oklahoma was way different than camping in New England. God would have to open doors quickly if we were going to survive the heat!

Henceforth, we determined, we would stick together and attend the three daily sessions of Campmeeting at the air-conditioned Tulsa Civic center. The meetings were incredible! It was like a dream to bask in the teaching of God's Word and be out of the heat.

After a morning session, offering time came. There was no pressure to give but a challenge to trust God with our finances. We were reminded of the promise in Luke 6:38, "Give, and it will be given to you: good measure, pressed down, shaken together, and running over will be put into your bosom. For with the same measure that you use, it will be measured back to you."

God was saying that if we would trust him in our giving, He would return to us through the hands of men an abundant supply to meet our every need. That is exactly the miracle we needed. At this point, we literally were down to $200. We reasoned that $200. was not enough to meet our needs. Only God could supply our needs now. It was not unlike the stories in the Bible where desperate people pushed through pride and fear and did desperate things to get to Jesus.

God delights to show Himself strong to those who are hungry for Him. II Chronicles 16:9a says, "For the eyes of the Lord run to and fro throughout the whole earth, to show Himself strong on behalf of those whose heart is loyal to Him."

Pam and I resolved to sow a financial seed of $100. Only those who's backs have been against the wall and who have thrown themselves completely upon Jesus can understand the mixed emotions accompanying such a move. On one hand, there was uncertainty and fear but at the same time there was a deep confidence and joyful expectation that the next move was in God's hands. He never disappoints!

The next day at Campmeeting, a gentleman approached me and Pam. He began to question us about where we were from and the nature of our business. We told him we were from Maine and would be attending Rhema Bible Training Center in September. Before stepping away, he handed me his business card and asked that we send our address when we were settled. He then tucked $200 into my shirt pocket. Each month while attending Rhema, he sent us $200 to $300 which essentially paid my school tuition.

The next big miracle we needed was a place to live. The only lead we had at this point was the phone number of the family who had posted at Oral Roberts University for domestic help. After prayer, we felt we should call them. Perhaps they knew someone looking for similar assistance.

After making contact by phone, we learned that the graduate couple they had hired could not come. Financial assistance had fallen through and therefor the position was again open. The next day we drove to their home to interview for the position.

The family lived off Lewis Avenue in an older but very nice home. Next door to them was the gated mansion of the heiress of Warren Oil Company and down the road was the home of Roy Clark. The evening we came for the interview, David, their youngest son was playing in the back yard.

As we pulled into the driveway, our son Justin immediately hopped out of the car and within minutes he and David were chasing each other around the gated yard. Justin and David were the exact same age and they immediately become fast friends.

As the boys played, Pam and I went inside and interviewed with the family. We sat in a spacious room surrounded with windows allowing us to see all the outside activity. Although the family was interested in me and Pam as a couple, it appeared they were more delighted in seeing that their youngest son had made a buddy. At the end of the interview, they offered us the position. Soon we would move from our tent into one of Tulsa's most prestigious neighborhoods with $100 to spare!

But from there you will seek the LORD your God, and you will find Him if you seek Him with all your heart and with all your soul.

Deuteronomy 4:29

Chapter 5
FROM TULSA TO TEXAS

The family had deep Tulsa roots. Steve, the dad, had grown up with Oral Roberts sons as playmates and Shirley was the president of the Junior League. We soon became acquainted with them and their three sons, Steve Jr., Jay Jay and David.

Pam, Justin and I lived in the garage apartment in the fenced in, tree surrounded yard. We were able to move into our quarters without spending a dime, but we still had immediate financial needs. We were living by faith, but the Bible says, ". . . do you want to know, O foolish man, that faith without works is dead?" - James 2:20.

I had seen an ad in the Tulsa World for a night security guard at one of the large petroleum companies in downtown Tulsa. After applying for the position, I was hired, handed a badge and 45-caliber pistol and assigned to roam the building all night. It was quick money, but I knew there had to be something better. This was just a stopgap measure until we got on our feet.

Soon I found another ad in the Tulsa World for a computer operator at a company called Strata Search. This company analyzed field data collected throughout Texas and Oklahoma where potential oil wells would be drilled. With my geology background, I figured this was a shoe in.

Sure enough, I was hired to work second shift. This was perfect because when school started in September, I would attend classes in Broken Arrow on Monday through Friday from 8am to noon. Then, I would return home, connect with family and head to downtown Tulsa to work from 3 to 11 PM.

Pam quickly bonded with Steve Jr., Jay Jay and David. Part of her responsibility was to help a few hours around the house each day. The boys gradually grew to love and respect her. Steve Jr. and Jay Jay attended private prep elementary schools. Pam treated them no different than we treated Justin. They were expected to eat what was prepared and clean up after themselves. The boys seemed to like and respect the discipline.

The first year was moving quickly and it seemed we had settled into our new life. One day, Shirley shared with Pam that Steve Sr. would be going for medical exams. He was preparing to take over his father's manufacturing business. The process required that he undergo comprehensive medical examinations for insurance purposes.

In the process of testing, Steve was found to have a serious heart condition requiring further examination. The decision was made for he and Shirley to travel to Texas where Steve would be seen by the world's leading heart physician at the time, Dr. Michael DeBakey.

Because both Steve and Shirley would be gone for an extended period for Steve's testing and possible subsequent procedures, Pam and I moved from the garage apartment into the main house. We were now primary guardians of the three boys.

Suddenly, our role shifted from outside hired help to surrogate parents and stewards of the household. Pam became acquainted with family and many of Shirley's friends. I began teaching a Bible study in the home of one of the friends of the family. We did our best to bring security and stability to the boys during this uncertain season.

One day the heartbreaking news was delivered that Steve had passed away in Texas following surgery. The boys would never again see their father. Shirley was devastated. Through this painful experience, Pam and I learned lessons of compassion and care for those facing tragedy. We learned to apply the Scriptural admonition of Romans 12:15 to, "Rejoice with those who rejoice, and weep with those who weep."

By God's grace we did our best to minister to Shirley and the boys as we entered the summer of 1980. Looking to the year ahead, we felt strongly the necessity for Pam to experience the teachings and environment of Rhema. Shirley graciously allowed us to shift times and responsibilities so that Pam would be able to attend the 1980-81 academic year at Rhema Bible Training Center.

This was one of the wisest decisions we could make. When God calls someone into ministry, if he or she is married, He calls their spouse too. The spouses' call may be for public or private ministry or it may simply be supportive by establishing a nurturing home. Regardless, it is essential that there be common understanding, love and commitment to the unique nature of the call. Amos 3:3 says, "Can two walk together, unless they are agreed?"

Together, during that second school year, Pam and I heard the Word from the many anointed staff teachers at Rhema. In addition, we heard from noted special guests such as Oral Roberts, Kenneth Copeland, Dr. Roy Hicks, Fred Price and Dr. Lester Sumrall. Each brought unique insights from the Word as well as a plethora of practical experience from which we would draw in the coming years.

During our first year in Tulsa, Pam and I had decided we would not discuss our move after graduation until we both had prayed and heard from God. We knew at some point the critical time would arrive for us to leave Tulsa and launch out into full time ministry.

Pam and I wanted to be certain that each of us had heard from heaven and that we were on the same page. This would be a major move and we determined to get it right. We both knew that there would be rough times ahead, and we both knew we needed to stay united. In the end, we were determined to live with the confidence of knowing we were in the center of God's will.

As the year was winding to an end, the time came for us to share the things God had placed in our hearts. So, we carved out private time and began the long-awaited conversation.

I said to Pam, "You go first." Immediately Pam began by saying, "All I know is that we are going to Pennsylvania." My jaw dropped. Then she said, "I just know it's somewhere in Pennsylvania." I then began to tell her my story.

My job at Strata Search had proved to be an ideal assignment. I would arrive each day at 3PM and connect with the day shift personnel. Usually, most of them left the office by 5PM at which time I was alone until 11PM operating the Hewett Packard computers.

Many jobs would run for hours at which time I was free to complete reading assignments, meditate upon the Word or to pray in the Spirit. To pray in the Spirit is to pray in the prayer language that accompanies the baptism in the Holy Spirit. This is a gift available to every born-again believer. It is the gift I had received four years earlier in the vacant apartment in Canastota, N.Y.

1 Corinthians 14:13–15 says, "For if I pray in a tongue, my spirit prays, but my understanding is unfruitful. What is the conclusion then? I will pray with the spirit, and I will also pray with the understanding. . ." The wonderful blessing of praying "in the Spirit" is that it supersedes the limitations of the natural mind. It positions one to tap into God's plans and purposes and then to walk in the light of them.

As Pam and I conversed, I shared with her how late one evening, while alone at work, I was praying in the Spirit. Suddenly, out of my spirit these words gently yet powerfully flowed, "When you finish school, move to Erie, become established and build a great church." At the time, I was not sure where Erie was located until I found it on the large world map hanging in the office. When I shared this with Pam, we both rejoiced at the confidence and certainty of knowing that we had heard from heaven!

Pam often jokes that I am the more spiritual of the two because she only got the state and I got the exact city. I smile at that, but I know beyond a shadow of doubt that the only reason Pam and I have been able to accomplish anything for God is because we are a team. Most husbands would do well to listen more closely to their wives. Proverbs 18:22 says "He who finds a wife finds a good thing and obtains favor from the Lord." I got the best!

We now knew where the Lord was sending us after graduation. Nevertheless, there was still some reluctance on our part. In the natural, we wanted to return to our home state, Maine to begin ministry. Our heads told us all the logical reasons to return. Maine needed a church that proclaimed the Word of Faith. Justin would be close to his grandparents. We loved the ocean and lakes, etc., etc. These were all rational thoughts with which to contend, but God had given us a scripture that put everything in proper perspective.

In prayer, the Lord had quickened to me Proverbs 19:21, "There are many plans in a man's heart, nevertheless the Lord's counsel—that will stand." People often dance around the God given answer for which they prayed because it is not what they want to hear.

Even after God gives the answer, we refuse to believe or act upon it. The problem is not that God did not hear or does not answer. The problem is we failed to take the time to prepare our hearts so that we can in earnest say, "Wherever He leads, I will follow." As a result, even when God gives the answer, we keep praying until we convince ourselves we have heard what we want to hear. That is a sure formula for confusion and disappointment.

That is exactly the situation Jeremiah the Prophet encountered when dealing with the remnant of Judah. They approached him requesting that he seek God on their behalf. Their request is found in Jeremiah 42:3, "That the Lord thy God may show us the way wherein we may walk, and the thing that we may do."

Because of disobedience, their land had been overthrown by the king of Babylon and they had already made up their mind that they wanted to desert the land and flee to Egypt. But, after ten days of prayer (v.7), the word of the Lord came to Jeremiah telling them to stay in the land and not flee to Egypt. That's not what they wanted to hear!

Jeremiah 42:20 (NLT) records the Prophets response to their disobedience. "For you were not being honest when you sent me to pray to the Lord your God for you. You said, 'Just tell us what the Lord our God says, and we will do it!'" Other translations render the passage, "for you were hypocrites in your hearts (NKJV); "for you showed yourselves perverse in your souls (YLT).

In other words, at the outset, they were not willing to obey the Lord's directives. They were just hoping He would put His seal of approval on their already made up minds and fixed plans.

All prayer begins with heartfelt submission to God. Jesus taught the model prayer in Matthew 6:10. It begins with, "Your kingdom come. YOUR will be done on earth as it is in heaven."

As Jesus began his ministry, Satan tried to distract him from God's purposes and plans by offering many alternatives (Matt 4:1-11). Throughout his earthly ministry, Jesus continually made decisions that went crosswise to his human desires and affinities. His life culminated with the great prayer he prayed in the garden before facing Calvary: "Father, if it is Your will, take this cup away from Me; nevertheless, NOT MY WILL, but Yours, be done" - Luke 22:42.

After working through these issues in our hearts, we set our face like flint to prepare for a move to Erie, Pennsylvania. One of the first things we did was to make a "confession sheet". This was simply a written statement of how we were releasing our faith. It was an affirmation of our faith in God and His promises to us. I can still remember it word for word:

"We know God's will, we walk in His perfect will and we have His wisdom. Our ministry is successful. We will reach one million people for Jesus Christ and we have $2000 to move. In Jesus name, Amen!"

We printed this faith confession on index cards and placed them on the bathroom mirror and on the dash of the Saab. We said it over and over to the point that Justin, our three and one half-year-old, would repeat it with us. We added the statement about the $2000 to move because we had no cash reserves to move to Erie. We were believing God for gas and travel money to get to our next assignment.

May and graduation time arrived and both Pam and I were greatly honored to stand in the Tulsa Civic Center with 422 other students as part of the Rhema graduating class of 1981. It was a joyful and meaningful moment to be handed our diplomas by Rev's Kenneth E. Hagin and Rev. Kenneth W. Hagin.

In a way, our entire family was graduating. Our son Justin was as much a part of this journey as me and Pam since his life had been greatly impacted during our two years in Tulsa. Part of our training included the things we learned at Rhema as well as in attending Faith Christian Fellowship, Pastored by Buddy and Pat Harrison. Pam had served in children's ministry at FCF under the tutelage of Willy George and I had served as a small group leader under the licensing umbrella of the church.

Periodically, during our time in Tulsa, we would correspond with the businessman in Texas who had placed the $200 check in my pocket at Campmeeting 1979. Each month, during our two years in Tulsa, he sent an unsolicited check that we used to cover our school tuition. It was a Godsend. Now, as we were preparing to leave Tulsa, he requested that we visit he and his family in San Antonio, Texas.

After prayer, we sensed this was the right thing to do. God had used this gentleman to bless us for two years. We felt it was proper to head 500 miles further south before going north to take time to thank him for his care and generosity. Plus, we were excited to see Texas!

Driving the secondary roads from Oklahoma to Texas was a great experience. The wide-open spacious plains were in stark contrast to the rocky coasts of Maine. We remember visiting the tiny country home where Lyndon Baines Johnson, America's 36th president grew up in Johnson City, Texas.

One especially memorable experience on this trip was the night we stayed in Hico, Texas. It was Friday evening, May 28, 1981. We remember the exact date because it was the eve of our 5th wedding anniversary. We pulled into the little town park of Hico where we met the local sheriff and asked him if there were any campgrounds in the area. Hico's motto is, "Where everybody is somebody." True to form, the sheriff quickly replied that we were welcome to camp out in the town park.

Although we felt somewhat exposed, we felt safe as we were acting on the sheriff's recommendation. So, we broke out our tent. About sundown, pickup truck after pickup truck pulled into the park and set up for a genuine Texas "hoedown". The entire experience was surreal. There was country music and square dancing and our tent was right smack in the middle of everything. We had a front row seat.

Finally, things settled down and we were able to get some sleep. We awoke the next morning, our 5th wedding anniversary, to the lowing of cows surrounding our tent. In recounting the experience, Pam has said this was not how she dreamingly anticipated our 5th wedding anniversary. I have been quick to remind her that we certainly made a memory! Soon we were on our way to San Antonio.

Mike and his family lived outside the city in a Texas ranch home they had built. We enjoyed going for walks around their spacious property and seeing rattle snakes and armadillos. We also enjoyed going into town and experiencing the mile-long river walk along the San Antonio river. Justin especially had fun at the Alamo and wearing his "Davey Crocket" hat. It was a wonderful experience filled with memories we still treasure.

The day came for us to say good bye and head towards Erie. Prior to leaving Tulsa, we had received a check for $300 from Sug and Lee. For over a year, we had taught a Bible study in their home and they wanted to bless us on our journey. With their gift and the $200 we had managed to save, we had $500 for our trip making us short by $1500 according to our confession of faith.

It is important to strongly emphasize that Pam and I never shared with anyone our confession of faith. This was a very personal and private matter between us and God. We were both mature enough to know and we had been taught to never use religious manipulation. True faith rests solidly upon God and His Word, not in subtle mind control or manipulation of people.

As we were leaving Mike and his family, Mike placed a check for $500 in my pocket. He and the family wanted to plant seed into our ministry and to bless us on our journey. We prayed and thanked them for their gracious hospitality and generous gift! We then got in the Saab to leave.

As we were pulling out of the driveway, Mike suddenly waved for me to stop and wait. He ran into the house and soon came out with another check which he placed in my hand. It was for $1000. He said God had spoken to him. God had again been faithful to fulfill His Word. We had $2000 for our move!

The wonderful thing about praying is that you leave a world of not being able to do something and enter God's realm where everything is possible. He specializes in the impossible. Nothing is too great for his almighty power. Nothing is too small for His love.

Corrie Ten Boom

Chapter 6
PLANTED IN ERIE

We headed straight east towards Louisiana for our next stop in New Orleans. There we would visit my old Coast Guard buddy, Dave Douglas. Dave and I shared many memories from our service days when we were assigned to the 378-foot Coast Guard Cutter, Hamilton stationed out of Boston, Massachusetts.

Together we had completed many Ocean Stations on the north Atlantic. These were 35-day trips sailing near Newfoundland and Greenland and at times playing cat and mouse with Russian ships. One special and more serious moment was when we passed the exact spot where the Titanic sank. We had made many of these journeys as well as annual trips to Guantanamo Bay, Cuba, better known as Gitmo.

On these trips, Dave, Kevin MacDonald and I jogged and worked out on the flight deck. When in port, we took every opportunity to visit the islands where we stopped for R&R. Together, we had jogged throughout Guantanamo Bay, Cuba, Jamaica, Haiti, Puerto Rico and the Virgin Islands. We made lots of memories and saw lots of sights.

Dave was now a business executive and he took the time to show us the

French Quarter and familiar sights of New Orleans. Our visit was short as Dave was busy and we were anxious to reach our new heavenly duty assignment in Erie, Pennsylvania.

Leaving New Orleans in the very early morning, we drove north crossing the 6-mile, I-10 Twin Span bridge over Lake Pontchartrain. Soon we were on I-59 North heading towards Birmingham and then on towards Nashville. We determined to drive straight through the 1100 miles to Erie. It was easier than stopping to pitch a tent and Justin slept soundly throughout the night.

Arriving in Erie during the early morning hours, we found a McDonalds on Peninsula Drive and were thrilled to get out of the car and finally stretch. As the sun rose in the east, we were struck with the exciting reality that we were home. What great and exciting things awaited us? What miracles would God perform as we continued to trust and obey Him? We were assured of God's promise found in Jeremiah 29:11, "For I know the thoughts that I think toward you, says the Lord, thoughts of peace and not of evil, to give you a future and a hope." The dream to, "Build a great church" was living large within our hearts!

After breakfast and time to freshen up, we began to "scope out" the region. We found Presque Isle state park just down the road from the McDonalds we visited. This beautiful park stretched out into Lake Erie and featured 11 miles of beaches. Driving around the park, we were comforted to once again be around water. Living two years in Oklahoma we often felt landlocked!

Our next mission was to find a place to pitch our tent. Just 3.5 miles south of the McDonalds where we stopped, we located a small private campground. Cassady's Campground was located on the west side of Erie on the banks of Walnut Creek, a large meandering stream. The campground was rustic, having passed it's prime, but it was very affordable.

By late afternoon we had set up camp on the banks of Walnut Creek.

We pitched our tent at what we thought was a safe distance from the water's edge. That night we would learn that Erie could experience dramatic downpours during the early summer season!

After bedding down for the night, it began to drizzle and then to pour. Pam and I were soon standing, holding up the tent as water gushed from the skies. Eventually Justin's little air mattress was floating on a stream running through our tent. When daybreak finally arrived, like Noah and his wife, Pam and I peeked out to see Walnut Creek swollen to inches of our tent door.

It was a night we will never forget and fortunately, Justin slept soundly through it all! It seemed we had crossed the "Red Sea" and come safely to the other side. Now began our long desert walk towards God's promises.

We had not been back home to Maine for two years and we felt it was important for us to connect with family before we became permanently established in Erie. So, after a few days of scouting out the region, we headed up to Maine. Although my parents could not fully understand their son's transformation, they were always supportive. Plus, we knew they were anxious to see their grandson!

God had amazing ways of always caring for us and answering prayer. He used my parents in one of those special ways while we were in Bible school. Every fall my parent's Catholic church held a raffle, and someone would win the big cash jackpot. During our first year in Bible school, my parents participated in the raffle and won the top prize of $700. They immediately sent us the money. The second year, they again participated and again won top prize! Again, they sent us the money. Year three the church barred them from participating!

Returning to Maine, we had a wonderful time reconnecting with family. While there, my parents graciously gave us their old pop-up travel camper to take back to the campground in Erie. No more streams running through the tent! After a week or so visit, we headed the 700 miles back to Erie.

Upon our return to Erie, we called home to report our safe arrival. We were greeted with the news that my father had suffered a heart attack. He was stable in the hospital and we were told to remain in Erie. My brother was there for family support. This was a devastating blow.

We also knew this was an attack from the enemy. One of the promises God had given to us was Matthew 19:29, "And everyone who has left houses or brothers or sisters or father or mother or wife or children or lands, for My name's sake, shall receive a hundredfold, and inherit eternal life." We knew this was likely brought on by my father's anxious concern for us. We also knew God's promise that He would reward our obedience to His call. Therefore, we were confident that my father would be ok. In fact, he was and as of this writing, both he and my mother are 92 years old.

God's specific directive to us was to, "Move to Erie, become established and build a great church." We were totally committed to the time element in completing this long-term assignment, therefore we knew the need for me to find employment so that we might "become established". From all economic indicators, that looked to be a major challenge.

Jimmy Carter had just left the Presidential office in January and America was struggling economically. Inflation drove mortgage interest rates as high as 21%. Companies were not hiring, and everything was "on hold".

While living in the campground, we had visited a local Assembly of God church located on Liberty Street in Erie. Standing in the foyer, a young man had caught my attention. He was wearing a brown polyester jacket identical to the one I owned. It was a jacket I recognized worn by ushers back in Tulsa.

As we exchanged greetings, we soon realized we had both recently graduated from Rhema Bible Training College in Tulsa! Kevin had returned to Erie, his hometown, and was teaching a Bible study in donated office space on Erie's east side. Both of Kevin's parents were assisting him.

Kevin's dad was nearing retirement having worked over 40 years at the local General Electric plant. This plant manufactured and shipped locomotives worldwide. Howard knew the pulse of the plant and how the current economic conditions adversely affected GE's hiring. Erie's unemployment rate was 12 to 14%. He knew things were locked up tight. Absolutely nobody was being hired. He had privately told Kevin my chances of finding employment at GE were slim to nothing.

Meanwhile, back at the campground, we were thanking God for favor. Faith is not moved by circumstances or economic conditions. Faith is only moved by God's Word. 2 Corinthians 5:7 says, "For we walk by faith, not by sight." Faith sees the promise and the answer and acts accordingly. So, we were confident that regardless of the economy, God would open doors on our behalf. After all, we were in Erie on His assignment! We were "all in" for God so we were confident He was "all in" for us.

While employed by Strata Search back in Tulsa, God had spoken to me at work one evening and said, "Learn the Hewett Packard computer system." Honestly, I had dismissed this premonition thinking that I would never again see Hewett Packard computers. After all, I was preparing to be a pastor-teacher-preacher of the Word! But God is much wiser than us and He can see around the corners where we are blind.

After a couple of weeks in the campground, I assembled my resume' and submitted it to a local employment agency. I soon heard back from them regarding an interview at the local G.E. plant. They were especially interested in me because of my experience with Hewett Packard computers! G.E. had just upgraded to the newest H.P. systems and they were looking for an experienced operator. I was hired on the spot! Again, God had given testimony to the power of prayer and His hand upon our lives. Soon we would be out of the campground!

In August, we moved from the campground to an apartment complex on Erie's east side. We were about to enter a season that would test our resolve.

The apartment was nice in appearance, but we soon learned of its issues. It was heated with radiant heat projected from the ceiling. This was extremely expensive to operate and rendered it impossible to stay warm during Erie's frigid winters. That winter, our son Justin became ill from the cold apartment and allergies triggered by the previous tenant's dogs. A combination of pneumonia and allergies sent Justin to the hospital for over a week.

In addition, our old Saab was getting tired. It was now 9 years old. It had taken me through the Coast Guard, college, my first job after college, Bible school in Oklahoma and delivered us to our assignment in Erie. One day the transmission died, and we were left without transportation.

Resigned to riding public transportation to work at GE, I would quietly listen to the morning conversations of shop workers as they chatted about the previous evening meal or their bowling league. In my mind, I would recount our preparations, purpose and calling. The devil would whisper to me, "Look at where you are. You are such a loser. All that preparation and here you are, riding the bus to work at a shop. You are hundreds of miles away from home and family and just wasting your life. Your wife and kid are stranded. Why don't you give up on this pipe dream!"

Satan would lay it on thick and I would have to remind myself of all that God had done in our lives and all He promised to do. It was not unlike when Jesus began his earthly ministry (Matthew 4:1-11). Satan threw everything he had at him. He wanted Jesus to doubt his call, to use his power selfishly and finally to yield to Satan's tyranny and just quit. But Jesus refused and in so doing he set a victorious example for every believer to follow!

James 4:7 reminds us to ". . . submit to God. Resist the devil and he will flee from you." During that season, we did not allow the immediate difficulties to quench the hope of our calling. We had learned how to encourage ourselves in the Lord (I Sam 30:6) and to believe the promise, "He who calls you is faithful, who also will do it" - I Thessalonians 5:24. With that resolve, we stayed the course believing that our best days were ahead.

We have found that when God is fully trusted, He is always faithful to fulfill His promises. At this point, we were assisting our friend Kevin with the Thursday evening Bible study. Mike, the business man who owned the building where the study was held, graciously offered us the use of his spare vehicle. It was a tremendous blessing. That act of kindness kindled hope in our hearts. It made clear how simple deeds done in love can make a huge difference in someone's life. It certainly did for us.

We continued assisting Kevin with the Bible study until January of 1982 when Kevin and I met at Elby's Restaurant on Broad Street on Erie's east side to discuss the formal establishment of a church. From that meeting, we began the process to incorporate Grace Fellowship International Church. Pam and I knew our calling to eventually plant a church on Erie's west side. However, we felt at this season, we had an opportunity to be a blessing by taking a supportive role.

Proverbs 15:33 says, "Before honor is humility." A key to promotion in God's Kingdom is the ability to show preference to one another. Many scriptures affirm this truth such as 1 Peter 5:6 which declares, "Therefore humble yourselves under the mighty hand of God, that He may exalt you in due time." It is not always easy to take second place, but it is always profitable to be promoted by the Lord in His due time.

Often, in haste, we make selfish decisions believing the end we desperately seek is justified by whatever means we employ. Someone feels called to a "great international ministry" but is unwilling to serve the immediate need in their local church. Another has a "passion for the lost" but is unkind towards their own spouse, the one they pledged to love and support. Another believes that God is "going to pour great abundance into their life" but they refuse to honor the Lord with their current tithe.

God expects us to be active and faithful with the immediate things before us. This is in stark contrast to being inactive and professing all we will do in the future. Jesus tells the parable about the good servant who was faithful in a small assignment and therefore was trusted with bigger responsibilities (Luke 19:17). As a wise ruler, God watches to see how we manage little matters before He entrusts us with greater responsibility.

Kevin, the Pastor, was a young single man with a strong call on his life. He needed stable support and encouragement, and at this season, we were happy to be there for him. Throughout the years, we have observed many young ministers struggle to succeed in ministry when they might have been more fruitful by taking second seat for a season and holding up the arms of another. We were happy to fulfill that role for a season.

Shortly after the incorporation of Grace Fellowship, the door opened for us to purchase a downtown church building that had recently closed. This was a huge financial step for us to take, but it formalized the presence of Grace Fellowship in Erie. We were excited to move from the temporary office space on Erie's east side into our own permanent location.

Kevin was able to devote himself exclusively to the oversight of the church while I continued working at General Electric. I eventually began to work 3rd shift so that I could do the work of ministry during the day. I was literally burning the candle at both ends. I would go to work at 11PM and operate computers until 7AM. As the sun arose in the morning, I would get a second wind driving home to begin a day filled with ministry related activity. It was a grueling season.

Many exciting things happened in the early years of Grace Fellowship.

Both Kevin and I had strong teaching gifts, therefore a ministry training school was incorporated as part of the church outreach. Faith Training Center reached people from all walks of life including three wonderful Catholic nuns who were hungry for the Word. We also hosted many notable guests including Dr. Lester Sumrall, Dr. Roy Hicks, Vicki Jameson Peterson and Pastor Tommy Reid.

One Sunday in early 1984, a few people who drove an hour each week from Titusville, PA to attend services at Grace Fellowship in Erie submitted a prayer request. They were hungry for a Spirit filled church to be planted in their home town. Titusville is a historic town that was placed on the map when Edwin L. Drake struck "rock oil" there in 1859. The discovery and subsequent drilling boom in Titusville literally shut down the east coast whale harvesting industry overnight. Drilled oil quickly replaced whale oil as a source of illumination in oil lamps.

When Pam and I saw the request, it immediately resonated in our hearts. We could continue to support the work of Grace Fellowship in Erie while we expanded the sphere and outreach of the Word of God to Titusville. After seeking the Lord's direction through prayer, Grace Fellowship Titusville began in April 1984.

The Bible says, "Do not despise these small beginnings, for the Lord rejoices to see the work begin. . ." - Zechariah 4:10 (NLT). Grace Fellowship Titusville began meeting at the Salvation Army building, 213 E Bloss Street. Soon, a storefront was rented, and the church began to grow. Pam and I always knew our call to Erie, PA. So, a year later, the church was placed into the capable hands of a young couple who had returned to Erie after graduating from Rhema Bible Training Center in Tulsa, Oklahoma.

It is easy to overlook the impact of a small work, but nothing done in faith, love and obedience to God's will is insignificant or small. From the Titusville church arose a powerful 17-year-old young man who today oversees an international network of churches and has done extensive work in the Ukraine training leaders and assisting the cause of democracy and freedom. Another young man who arose from the Titusville church went on to lead international teams to rescue women and children from slavery around the world. Other pastors and leaders developed from the Titusville church. The current pastor of the church regularly travels to Africa to train leaders.

The Word of God says, "For we walk by faith, not by sight", II Corinthians 5:7. We have been in ministry long enough to see the amazing fruits of small beginnings done in faith, love and obedience.

After transitioning leadership of the Titusville church, we began a radio and teaching ministry. The radio broadcast, "Rise and Be Healed" was heard daily on WCTL Radio, 106.3 FM. Twice a week we met at the historic St. John Kanty Prep building where we conducted, Prayer and Healing School. Eventually we rented a storefront on 837 West 38th Street where we held our Prayer and Healing School. People from many denominations and church backgrounds came to hear the Word of God regarding the subjects of faith, healing and the authority of the believer. Of course, Jesus was always at the center of our teaching.

It was always our desire to impart books and faith building materials into people's hands to help them grow spiritually. The Bible says in Hosea 4:6, "My people are destroyed for lack of knowledge." We knew the powerful difference accurate spiritual knowledge made in our lives. Therefore, we felt indebted to share the same with others.

After renting the storefront, I gave Pam $100 of seed money to purchase books, music and other faith building material. The man who owned the storefront agreed to build a wall dividing the store. We had about 450 sq. feet of space up front for Faith Bible Bookstore and the remaining 1600 sq. feet was set up as a teaching center.

The landlord was an older Italian gentleman who "took a liking" to us because of our entrepreneurial spirit. His wife had passed away and he had two sons who were both attorneys. He especially liked Pam because, "she reminded him of his deceased wife."

One day he told Pam his story. His parents were both Italian immigrants to the United States. As a young teenager, he came home and proudly told them that he had found employment. His mother's surprising response was, "If you are going to work for someone else, you are going to live somewhere else." He shared how this quickly turned him into a self-starter and entrepreneur! At this point, he owned multiple buildings including the complex which housed the store he rented to us.

After we had rented from him for years and never missed a rental payment, he one day told us this story. He said, "I was prepared to carry you for six months if you could not make the rental payment. I learned you have to return back what has been given to you." He said, "I was given breaks that enabled me to succeed. When I see others striving to realize a dream, I am compelled to help them."

God used this aged Italian gentleman to help us accomplish our dream. This kind man had certainly done well financially, yet he drove an old panel van with orange hubcaps. There was more substance to him than flash. But God used him to answer our prayer.

And the LORD restored Job's losses when he prayed for his friends. Indeed, the LORD gave Job twice as much as he had before.

Job 42:10

Chapter 7
BUILDING A GREAT CHURCH

During the next season, we supported the ministry of Grace Fellowship while I continued to work at General Electric, produced daily radio programs and conducted our Prayer and Healing School. Pam developed the bookstore and significantly increased its inventory. She did that by continually reinvesting every penny from sales to purchase additional inventory. Of course, that required moving the wall several times to expand the store. Eventually, the book store took over the entire floor space. Pam seldom took a paycheck, but we paid all our employees.

God had been dealing with us about the assignment we received when He sent us to Erie: "Move to Erie, become established and build a great church." I had now worked at G.E for 7 years. This was way longer than I ever expected. I was dragging my feet to plant another church because I did not want to appear in any way divisive. We had continued to support to work of Grace Fellowship, but the time had come for us to fulfill our specific assignment.

After much prayer and dialogue with Kevin, Pam and I made the decision to begin Erie Christian Fellowship Church. My supervisors at G.E. had previously given me "the talk" about the pathway to promotion at G.E. I had stepped away from pursuing that career path because we were committed to the call of God. We did not leave home and family and careers and come to a strange city so that we could go back to living "a normal" lifestyle.

Kevin was most gracious in sending us off to begin our new work on Erie's west side. At this point, I had left G.E. and was unemployed. We began to search for the right place to begin. Finally, we settled on a former public-school building that had been purchased by a private Montessori school. This building was located on the main road we traveled 8 years previously when we first arrived in Erie. It was approximately 3 miles from where we had pitched our tent on the banks of Walnut Creek.

In making a firm decision to move ahead with the church, we quickly learned how the devil is subtle and uses every means both overt and covert to hinder the work of God. At this point, I had been away from G.E. for about 6 months and our personal finances were unraveling. In fact, we were a month behind with our mortgage payment. Yet, we had made the decision that "live or die, sink or swim, we were moving forward with our assignment in Jesus' Name!" I was through working a secular job. We were moving into full time ministry!

I had gone to the Montessori school to sign a lease on the property and returned to the bookstore to celebrate with Pam. Personal money pressures loomed, and now we had a lease and no assurance of what finances could be expected from the new church. As I walked into the bookstore, Pam immediately said, "G.E. just called and they want you to come back to work."

If we had not understood the power of resolve and commitment and been confident that we were obeying God's plan, we may have taken the bait. We had learned to be led by God's Spirit and not by open and closed doors. Romans 8:14 says, "For as many as are led by the Spirit of God, these are sons of God."

Every open door is not a door God has opened. On the other hand, some closed doors are meant to be kicked open. It is critical to understand the subtle difference. Matthew 11:12 says, ". . . the kingdom of heaven suffers violence, and the violent take it by force." We were in a "take it by force" mode at this point. That phone call was not a blessing from heaven in disguise. Rather, it was the Pharaoh of this world saying, "It's OK to serve God, but don't go out too far. Don't get too radical. Just stay at GE and be safe" (Exodus 8:28).

I certainly am not opposed to a minister working a secular job to make ends meet. The Apostle Paul did that. I did it for 7 years helping to plant 2 churches. However, in our case, we knew that season was over. I had gladly sowed my life and paid my dues. We knew we were not acting with presumption in taking this stand. We were standing in faith, putting pressure on God's Word. We were doing what He sent us to do. That took the entire pressure off us.

I immediately called G.E. and said, "'Thank you, but I am not available". We then began plans for the first service of Erie Christian Fellowship Church at the Montessori School, 2910 Sterrettania Road. That service was scheduled for July 9, 1989.

It was not until Good Friday, 30 years later that I realized the significance of that specific day. More than ever, we are aware of how God works silently to guide and govern His affairs in the earth. In Acts 2:23, Peter speaks of, "the determined purpose and foreknowledge of God".

Woven through the tapestry of men's actions and decisions, both evil and good, God works to silently fulfill His determined purposes. One of the hallmark messages of our life and ministry is the atoning work of Jesus Christ. Peter tells us, "Who Himself bore our sins in His own body on the tree, that we, having died to sins, might live for righteousness— by whose stripes you were healed" - I Peter 2:24. Jesus is God's atoning Gift to provide forgiveness and healing for all!

In the Old Testament, the Great Day of Atonement began on the evening of the 9th until the evening of the 10th day of the 7th month (Leviticus 23:32 v27). I understand our Gregorian calendar does not correspond with the Jewish calendar. However, I am amazed that Erie Christian Fellowship began exactly on the date corresponding to the Great Day of Atonement, the ninth day of the seventh month – July 9, 1989.

Our only advertising was to place a single small ad in the Erie Daily Times promoting the first service. We had about 50 plastic chairs from our Prayer and Healing School that we set up in the gymnasium. For sound we had a small Radio Shack amplifier I used for radio production and a half dozen "sing-along" cassette tapes for worship music. The Saturday afternoon before our first service (and for months thereafter), I spent two hours mopping and dusting grip chalk from the auditorium left by the Saturday morning girl's gymnastics class.

With the arrival of Sunday morning, we were excited and ready to go! Justin, now 12 years old, was our first usher. He greeted people at the door and handed out bulletins. Pam led worship, exhorting people to sing along with the prerecorded songs on the cassette tape. Forty-six people attended that first service.

I remember glancing toward the entry door as the service began. In walked a crisp, professional looking couple who briskly took their plastic seats. The thought immediately ran through my head, "You'll never see them again." But friends, the devil is a loser and a liar. That thought was not from God. It did not proceed from my spirit. Rather it was a thought the devil planted in my head because of my concern of our crude facilities at that point.

Hanging on the upper walls of the gym were old yellowing gymnastic posters. On the platform was a tattered stage curtain that fell short to reaching the floor by two feet. And, as I said, at this point the church staff consisted of Pam, Justin and me. We were all volunteers.

It is important to know how faithful the Lord is to work with those who courageously represent His cause. Mark 16:20 says, "And they went out and preached everywhere, the Lord working with them . . ." The Lord was working with us that day by sending a faithful couple who became founding members of Erie Christian Fellowship Church. Phil and Sandi had just arrived in Erie where Phil was the new manager of a manufacturing plant that produced chemical catalyst for worldwide distribution.

Phil and Sandi were empty nesters and anxious to assist with a full gospel start up church. Although Phil's job had just brought them to Erie, their passion was the work of the ministry. The previous day they had just read our newspaper ad and showed up at our first service. Phil went on to become one of our first financial board advisors as well as a keyboard player on our worship team. Sandi became a major leader in our prayer ministry. One of our church's first small group met in their home.

Another attendee at our first church service was Diane who had been one of the first attendees at Prayer and Healing school. She and her mother were hungry to grow in the Word of God. Diane was teaching in the public-school system. She eventually became our first Children's Pastor and the founding principal of our Christian School, Leadership Christian Academy.

Two other attendees at the first service, Camille and her husband Tim, were public school teachers. Camille taught elementary school for over 30 years, but her primary passion was missions. When she retired from teaching in 1997, she immediately became our mission's director. Over the years she was responsible for coordinating and sending scores of people on short term mission trips.

As I ponder the early days of Erie Christian Fellowship, I am deeply aware of God's faithfulness. To anyone beginning a new endeavor I would say, pray and be certain your motives are pure. Psalm 37:5 says, "Commit your way to the Lord, trust also in Him, and He shall bring it to pass." The Lord will work with you, granting you favor and assistance. But, when He calls you to a work, He also calls you to help and empower others who, along with you, have giftings and dreams in their hearts. If he can trust you to be a good and faithful steward and a responsible and respectful leader, He will bless and increase the work.

Our second advisory board member and attendee at ECF's first service was a man we affectionately called, "the gentleman from Lake City". John and his wife Kakie were grape farmers. John had been filled with the Holy Spirit and turned on to the teaching of God's Word. John was a silver haired and stately looking WWII Marine who always wore a blue blazer when he was not in farming overalls. He and Kakie hailed from Lake City, PA., hence, he was nicknamed, "the gentleman from Lake City".

About two months after the church began, another couple, Paul and Lewanna visited one Sunday morning. They had left Erie *for* Tulsa, Oklahoma the same summer we had arrived in Erie *from* Tulsa in 1981. Back in 1981, Paul's successful building business had folded when mortgage interest rates had soared to 21%. Suddenly Paul was shackled with unmovable home inventory and bank loans that quickly devoured all profits. He had no choice but to turn their inventory over to the bank.

Paul grew up on a farm in Erie and, as a young teenager, committed his life to Jesus. His mother was a Four-Square minister who during the 60's (with the family's blessing) left the farm and family to receive a semester of Bible training at A.A. Allen's Miracle Valley Bible School in Arizona. Paul had many stories of his mother's faith in action such as the time she stayed the rain until all the crops were harvested.

Amid the economic downturn of 1981, Paul realized it was time for him to get greater and more accurate teaching from God's Word. He and his family had moved to Tulsa, Oklahoma where they could be in the environs of Kenneth Hagin Ministries and Rhema Bible Training Center. After owning his own building business in Erie, Paul picked up a hammer and began to work as a house framer in Tulsa for $6.00 an hour. Paul was not afraid to work. And, Paul knew, with God the only way to go was up!

After living and growing spiritually in Tulsa for eight years, he and his family had just returned to Erie. They were hungry to continue their spiritual growth and they were looking for a church of the flavor they had experienced in Tulsa. Specifically, they were looking for a church with teachings in accord with Romans 10:8, "But what does it say? 'The word is near you, in your mouth and in your heart' (that is, *the word of faith which we preach)*". That is what Pam and I had experienced in our personal lives and it was the manner of teaching that had transformed our lives.

Now, in 1989, after returning to Erie, Paul made inquiry as to "whether there were any churches in the area teaching faith". Someone told him, "There is a fellow by the name of Jim Dumont who teaches faith on the radio". That was like saying "sic'em!" to a dog. Paul and Lewanna and their family were soon attending services at Erie Christian Fellowship at the Montessori School. It was my honor to conduct the funeral for Paul's dear mother who passed away just weeks after Paul and Lewanna's return to Erie. And, Paul soon became our third church advisory   board   member.

You can do more than pray after you've prayed, but you cannot do more than pray until you've prayed. Prayer is striking the winning blow; service is gathering up the results.

S.A. Gordon

Chapter 8
FRESH PAINT AND MEN IN BLACK

Jesus says in Revelation 21:5, "Behold, I make all things new." We are not to lightly esteem the day of small beginnings. We began in an environment to which our school landlords had grown accustomed. They were doing their best with what they had. On the other hand, we knew it was incumbent upon us to do all within our power to rightly represent Jesus. So, we quickly went to work making things fresh and new!

Soon we had renegotiated the rent in exchange for our out of pocket investment to replace the stage "shower curtain" with a full-length grand drape with borders. The entire gymnasium was repainted by our church crews and down came the yellowed and torn posters. Things were looking good!

We then moved towards the basement. My attention immediately focused on an old storage room that held the possibility of church office space. Our neighbor, Rick, whom we had led to faith in Jesus, was an expert framer. He along with other men turned that tired dingy space into a beautiful secretary's office and Pastor's study.

Soon Joyce, our first worship leader, joined us and we were forever free from the canned cassette worship tapes. O happy day!

It is important to emphasize God's faithfulness to work alongside with those representing His cause by preaching the good news of the gospel. The Scripture says in II Corinthians 6:1, we are ". . . workers together with Him. . ." That means God is fully committed to partner with and to supernaturally augment and amplify the efforts of those who proclaim the gospel. One might say He puts His "super" upon our natural efforts.

On the second Sunday of November 1990, I had just begun to preach when two professional looking men slipped in and sat in the back row of the gymnasium. They immediately caught my attention. One was Caucasian and the other African American and both were well groomed wearing crisp suits and ties. The whole time I preached, in the back of my mind, I wondered "who are those men?" This predated the movie, "Men in Black", but imagine the likes of Will Smith and Tommy Lee Jones walking in out of nowhere. I was thinking the IRS or agents of some government or ecclesiastic entity were here to check us out!

At the end of the service they lingered and introduced themselves to me. One was Rev. Bill Young, a Rhema Bible Training Center graduate who was helping his father-in-law with a small Apostolic inner-city church he had long ago established on Erie's lower east side. The other gentleman was Rev. Robin Roberts, also a Rhema Bible graduate who lived in Tulsa, Oklahoma.

Rev. Roberts had prayed, and the Lord had specifically directed him to travel from his home in Tulsa, Oklahoma to Erie, PA. There he met Rev. Young who in turn introduced him to his father in law. Robin had been conducting special services at the church of Rev. Young's father in law. Since their Sunday service did not begin until 12:30 PM, Rev Young brought Robin to Erie Christian Fellowship to meet me.

From that first meeting began a longstanding friendship and ministry relationship. Before attending Bible school, Robin had been a successful executive overseeing multiple business enterprises. When called by God, like Elisha, he and his wife (with their three young daughters) abandoned professional aspirations to boldly pursue God's call and plan for their life.

People often wonder how one can know the genuineness of a man or woman of God. In my conversations with Robin, it came to my attention that while in Erie, he had been residing as a guest with a family in a modest and crowded home with three teenage children. His room was chilly. In fact, while preparing messages, he would sit on his hands attempting to stay warm.

As his ministry time in Erie was winding down, I offered to host him in a hotel where he would be much more comfortable and enjoy a measure of solitude. Robin respectfully declined knowing that to transition from his present accommodations would disrespect and possibly offend his hosts. Of course, I understood, but this insight gave me clear indication of Robin's character. He was more concerned for people than personal comfort or gain. Robin was the real deal; a true man of God.

I asked him to preach for us at the end of his current commitment. He agreed and on the fourth Sunday of November 1990, Robin Roberts conducted his first meeting at Erie Christian Fellowship. It was a blessing both for Robin and for our church. The generosity of our congregation made up for his financial deficiencies. Robin had faithfully and lovingly continued preaching the Word at his previous venue despite the congregation's inability to meet his modest financial needs.

Robin personally shared with me that his first offering had been $12.15 in cash. The most he received in any offering never exceeded $95. Robin said, "I just trusted my Lord Jesus!" Robin told me during his second visit to ECF, during a time of prayer, the Lord spoke to him and said, "Help Pastor Jim in any way possible he may ask." I am humbled that Robin, in recounting this story, shared with me the following: "To date, I have endeavored to fulfill that Heavenly mandate! I consider it one of my highest callings!"

As our relationship developed, Robin eventually became a corporate board member of Erie Christian Fellowship Church. Every November for multiple years, it was our longstanding tradition to have Robin preach a week of special miracle meetings. Many people were born again, filled with the Holy Spirit and healed during these annual meetings. Robin's prophetic insight was quite remarkable. He prophesized to us the birth of our second grandchild before we had any knowledge of his conception.

God's calling and assignment to me and Pam had been to, "Move to Erie, become established and build a great church". To us, "a great church" meant a place where Jesus would be exalted, and people would be spiritually established in the Word of faith. It also meant building a physical campus to house our congregation and facilitate education and outreach.

To that end, we knew it was necessary that we find a permanent location for our church. Through prayer and the Holy Spirit's leading, we were certain of our call to Erie's west side. That is why we gratefully but respectfully declined when an elderly couple in our congregation offered to give us land located in another area of town. We knew if we remained obedient to God's specific directives, He would provide for every need. Believe me, it was difficult to say "No thank you" to such a generous offer.

Natural reason and logic can quickly lead to confusion if they lead one to deviate from God's revealed will. Deuteronomy 29:29 says, "The secret things belong to the Lord our God, but those things which are revealed belong to us and to our children forever, that we may do all the words of this law." That simply means we do not know or understand everything. There are secrets that belong only to God. That is His prerogative. He is certainly not obligated to tell us everything.

However, there are things God desires to make very clear to us. When He does, we are wise to act in accord with His revealed will. The Apostle Paul said in Acts 26:9, "Indeed, I myself thought I must do many things contrary to the name of Jesus of Nazareth." That was Paul's natural reasoning and logic controlling his actions and behavior before he came to personally know Jesus.

Reason told him to fight, persecute and destroy the early church. But, when Jesus arrested him on the Damascus Road, Paul had enough spiritual sense to say, "I was not disobedient" - Acts 26:19. Paul's obedient submission to Jesus transformed him from being a destroyer to a builder of people and many churches!

Romans 12:2 says, "And do not be conformed to this world, but be transformed by the renewing of your mind, that you may prove what is that good and acceptable and perfect will of God." Study of God's Word, sincere prayer and obedience are vital if one is to walk in line with God's perfect will.

Eventually, we created a "confession of faith" like the one we wrote out and affirmed when preparing to leave Tulsa. This one, however, affirmed, ". . . we have property on Sterrettania Road on Route 832. . ." That was a bold statement, but we were confident of Jesus' promise in Matthew 19:26, "With men this is impossible, but with God all things are possible." We knew that prayer always worked!

It was November 1991 and we still operated Faith Bible Bookstore. Through the store, Pam had lots of interaction with Erie's Christian community at large. Every Thanksgiving and Christmas season, shoppers flooded the isles as WCTL, Erie's Christian radio station broadcasted live from our store. Faith Bible Bookstore became a hub of activity for the greater Erie region.

One day, a real estate lady Pam knew stopped in. As she and Pam visited, Pam shared about the church and things happening. When Pam mentioned our search for land, the lady excitedly told her about a family member who owned property on Sterrettania Road (Rt 832).

This was exactly the area we were targeting! The lady offered to talk to her relative on our behalf regarding sale of the property. Returning a few days later, she recounted that a portion of the land had been sold to the school district. There the township would build an elementary and middle school. Additionally, across the street, her relative planned to develop a large subdivision. However, he agreed to sell the corner lot opposite to where the schools would be built. This land would be surrounded by the new subdivision.

Our purchase price for this 7.7 acres of prime real estate was $105,000. Additionally, the owner agreed to hold the mortgage. This was important because, at this point, our church had yet to establish credit with any bank. After rallying, the church retired the ten-year note in 18 months! Immediately adjoining our new property was the only remaining piece of undeveloped land in the area, a privately owned four-acre farm. Nothing indicated the imminent availability of this property.

However, in my spirit, I knew we must acquire this land. During planning meetings with our church board, we would pray, and I would remind them that if (and when) the farm became available, we must purchase it. Two years later, on a Monday morning in January 1994, as I drove around the corner, I was amazed to see a "for sale" sign planted in front of the farm adjacent to our land.

Heading straight to my office, I immediately called the listing realtor and got the specifics. The land had been subdivided into three separate parcels. The farmhouse with two acres and two, one acre lots. The combined price for everything was $150,000.

This is where preparation proved critical for us. Because of prayer and our previous board discussions, we were able to move quickly. I called Phil who was in Europe on a business trip and his immediate response was, "buy it"! All other board members said the same. I was given total freedom to move quickly on this opportunity. We knew this window would close quickly.

Tuesday morning, I met with the realtor to discuss our purchase of the property. Wednesday morning, we signed intent to purchase papers and submitted a deposit. The first viewing of the property was not scheduled until Friday evening when multiple agents lined up with their clients anxious to tour the property. All were disappointed (and some quite angry) to know that the property had already been sold.

This would not have happened if we had not with foresight prayed and maintained vigilance. Had our board lacked unity, vision and faith, the opportunity would easily have slipped through our hands. One week later we held our first prayer meeting in the farmhouse which would eventually become valuable office and meeting space. This was a time to rejoice!

One of the greatest aspects of prayer is it brings you up into His presence and, His perspective is vastly different.

Unknown

Chapter 9
BEYOND OUR FOUR WALLS

Amid our leading, pastoring and building plans, God was still moving forward with His primary agenda to bring the gospel to the entire world. After all, Jesus' final directive to His church was to, "Go into all the world and preach the gospel to every creature" - Mark 16:15. That agenda has never changed.

One day, as I was alone praying in the Montessori school basement, from within my spirit, I clearly heard these words, "Greater realms and spheres of influence. . . pray for it, believe it and expect it." As with all directives from the Lord, if they do not presently make sense, it is best to put them on a shelf in one's heart and to ponder the message. And, that's what I did. At the same time, I began with regularity to pray in line with the directive, asking God for "Greater realms and spheres of influence."

I went about my daily activities. One afternoon, I received a phone call from someone with an African accent. He asked if he could meet and speak with me. I was quite suspicious because pastors receive all manner of calls from sales people to travelers in need of gas money to outright scams. Everyone wants to get through because the common thought is the pastor is the one person who can make final decisions.

As I listened with my heart to this gentleman, I sensed a genuine humility and sincerity about him. So, I cautiously agreed to meet at the local motel where he was staying. When we met, he told me he was from Nigeria and that he had oversight of numerous churches. In addition, he was the presiding bishop of IPMF, the International Pentecostal Ministers Fellowship in Nigeria.

This all seemed quite fantastic and difficult to believe. However, he was familiar with Kenneth E. Hagin and Rhema Bible Training College, the school from which we graduated in Tulsa, Oklahoma. He lovingly referred to brother Hagin as "Papa Hagin". As we spoke, I could tell he was truly a man of faith. He had written several books and one that immediately caught my eye was, "Why the Way of Faith?" His ministry was called "Faith Productions" and ours was "Faith Communications". Tim Obidike and I were becoming fast friends.

The thing that clinched for me the genuineness of Rev. Tim Obidike was he never subtilty or overtly asked anything of me. He sincerely was seeking my friendship and I could tell this was a God moment. Previously, I have spoken of the litmus test that proved to me the sincerity of Rev. Robin Roberts. Insight into his character allowed me to trust him. The same was true with Bishop Tim Obidike.

He shared with me his story of how he was born the son of a fetish priest and how, as a child, he literally slept on the dirt floor of a hut with snakes. He had been introduced to the Gospel through books authored by Kenneth E. Hagin. After committing his life to Christ, he was told by everyone in his community that he would never amount to anything or have a wife because he would be unable to collect the necessary dowry. By becoming a Christian, he had, in their estimation chosen a powerless path of poverty and defeat. By turning his back on his father's idols, he had sealed his fate.

Choosing, however, to believe the Word of God, Tim began making bold declarations of faith that he would one day fly in an airplane and most certainly have a wife. He became the first person in his village to own a bicycle and at the time of our initial meeting, he was a proud husband and father of 5 sons. And, he had traded in his bicycle for an automobile! Obviously, he had flown in an airplane to come to the United States. As Tim would often say, "Faith Works!"

Knowing the importance of world missions, I invited Tim to share on a Sunday morning and our relationship was forged. Tim was a powerful teacher of the Word with a delightful sense of humor. His combination of humility, bold confidence in Christ and funny African stories gave beautiful expression of the gospel. Tim won the hearts of our congregation who were delighted to experience God's amazing orchestration of a divine connection just as we read in the book of Acts.

Over the years, Tim made numerous trips to the United States and, we as well, made three trips to Nigeria. During our first two trips, we conducted ministers training seminars. It was always a delight to assemble national pastors and leaders who seldom had the opportunity to participate in a minister's conference. We would bring Bibles, notebooks, training materials and pens which were treasured items. Many of the pastors received their first Bible at these seminars. In addition, Erie Christian Fellowship generously purchased land and materials for a church in Enugu, Nigeria.

In 2000, we planned our biggest trip to impact the leaders of Nigeria. Through my daily radio broadcast and Faith Bible Bookstore, we announced our goal to collect new or gently used leather bound Bibles. These would be distributed at our Leadership Training Seminar in Nigeria. We successfully gathered 14 large boxes filled with beautiful leather Bibles.

We called ahead and coordinated with the airline in Pittsburgh to accommodate our additional baggage. The day we arrived, the airline told us we would have to fly separate from our boxes. This was an impossible arrangement because at the time, the Lagos, Nigeria airport was notorious as one of the worst airports in the world. It was swarming with con men and criminals waiting to prey on unsuspecting travelers. There was no way we would be reunited with our Bibles if we were separated from them.

We waited and prayed as the airline went to work to figure things out. Close to an hour later, they summoned us to offer a solution. To fly with our boxes, they would first fly us to Dallas, Texas. There, they would put us on a different flight where we would fly with all our Bibles. We would arrive in Lagos one hour later than originally planned. And, providing we were agreeable, they would upgrade our entire party to first class!

We were soon to learn the surprises for this trip had just begun. Arriving in Nigeria, we were united with Rev. Tim and drove the 9 hours from Lagos to Enugu. I could tell something was different on this trip. Tim was quiet. We did not immediately discuss the conference plans as typically we would do. Arriving in Enugu, he sat us down with our British associate from London, Rev. D.P. French, to tell us why.

Gasoline prices had spiked making transportation difficult for pastors. Besides that, there was another situation that took precedence over the conference. Over the previous year, an area where Tim's ministry had sponsored a mission outreach (Umuleri in Amambra, State) had experienced tribal war. Over 115 people had been killed and bodies laid unburied for months. Properties had been burned and destroyed with dynamite. Ashamed and afraid, people had scattered and not returned to the area. Tension and shame pervaded the atmosphere throughout the entire region.

After prayer, Tim felt strongly that something must be done. Just as I had once trusted Tim, he was confident I would trust him again with the modified agenda for this trip. He had already moved ahead with plans to reunite the entire region. He had coordinated a tribal reconciliation ceremony where the tribal leaders and residents of the region would come together and we, as ministers of the gospel, would minister peace and reconciliation to the region. We all agreed to this plan.

Soon fear inspired rumors spread that the Americans had arrived with bombs to finish off the conflict. Tim knew we must move quickly to quench this rumor. We soon had an idea. A single box filled with our Bibles was sent ahead to the community with a note saying, "These are the bombs the Americans brought. Come to the reconciliation ceremony and let God bring peace in Jesus Name."

The day of the ceremony, tension was high as we arrived in Umuleri. There, we were met by military personnel and informed that, scattered throughout the woods, were soldiers with weapons. They were there to insure no flare ups occurred. That day, more than ever, we had an awareness of the importance and power of our callings as ambassadors of Christ.

The event transpired without incident. We preached on Jesus' mission to bring peace, reconciliation and forgiveness. Each leader was prayed for and the traditional Kola nut was shared. At the completion of the ceremony, our Bibles were distributed to all the tribal leaders.

This was an amazing experience that demonstrated to us the importance of being open and flexible in mission work. It also showed us the power of influence each of us carry. In our humble service, we were perceived as powerful American ambassadors. It made us keenly aware of the meaning of Romans 10:15 "And how shall they preach unless they are sent? As it is written: 'How beautiful are the feet of those who preach the gospel of peace, Who bring glad tidings of good things!'"

We have learned how God works in line with His Word and in response to our faith. Our vision has always been to impact, train and empower the coming generation with the Word of God. Towards that end, we placed a high value on Children and Youth ministry.

After faithfully serving as a volunteer for many years in our Children's ministry, Diane Price was eventually employed as our first Children's Pastor. Once our dynamic Children's ministry was up and running, Diane and I prayed and discussed the formation of a Christian School.

Over the years, Diane and I had many laughs over the things we did without knowing how to do them. We would pray, then jump right in taking first steps, trusting God to provide the wisdom and necessary resources.

By 2012, Leadership Christian Academy was up and running. In fact, we were short on class space as we attempted to accommodate all grades from Pre-K through grade eight. Our School board had many lengthy discussions trying to "figure" a solution. We would go around and around and eventually land at the same spot. We were way short on funds necessary to undertake a third building program.

One afternoon, I was scheduled to address parents and teachers to discuss our situation. Before addressing the group, I prayed asking the Lord for wisdom in what to say. I felt strongly impressed to share the miracle found in all four gospels where Jesus fed over 15,000 people (5,000 men plus women and children) with a young boy's lunch consisting of 5 loaves and 2 small fish (Matt 14:17).

Standing before the assembly, I talked about the many miracles Jesus performed. I shared how Jesus placed a priority on children and recounted how Jesus only needed a little with faith to produce a lot. One little boy had enough faith in Jesus to surrender his entire lunch. From that, Jesus performed an amazing miracle of provision!

When I was done speaking, I simply asked if anyone would like to give in faith towards the huge miracle we needed. People had not come prepared to give, but one lady in the group responded. I watched as Holly Bowers eagerly dug through her purse until she found the only cash she had on hand, a five-dollar bill.

Holding up the bill, I followed Jesus' example in blessing it and the people. I thanked Him for the miracle He was about to perform. Time passed quickly, and parents needed to pick up their children, so I dismissed the meeting.

Most people had left the room when an elderly gentleman whom I had never seen approached me with his hand extended. I reached out and he placed something in my hand for which I thanked him. Immediately he left the room.

When everyone was gone, I opened my clasped palm to see two crumpled dollar bills he had placed there. I am somewhat embarrassed to admit, that, upon seeing the two crumpled bills, my immediate thought was identical to that of Andrew's. When looking at the five loaves and two small fish he blurted out, "But what are they among so many?" - John 6:9. At least, I had the composure to keep my mouth shut.

And then . . . it dawned on me. Wait a minute! Five loaves and two small fish. . . a five-dollar bill and two one-dollar bills! What was God doing?

The following week, out of the blue, the school secretary received a phone call from her brother in Ohio. He worked construction and he wondered if, by chance, our school had any need of two portable class buildings? An Ohio public school had utilized the mobile units during construction of additional space. If we wanted them, we could have them for one dollar each! We would just have to move them off the property.

The story doesn't end there. That same week Don Johnson, our facilities director, was walking our church property when two dollars blew across his path. He immediately gave the money to the school and ever since has humorously claimed that he paid for the school's new portable units.

When word was communicated to our church and school about the class units, many people pitched in. One of our school board members sent a crew of workers to Ohio to pick up and deliver the units to our property. We hustled and were able to acquire all the necessary permits. Businesses associated with our church and school donated materials and labor towards the restoration and renewal of the units. When all was said and done, we had two beautifully restored portable units – each housing two spacious classrooms. God had responded to our need and answered our prayer!

Call to Me, and I will answer you, and show you great and mighty things, which you do not know.

Jeremiah 33:3

Chapter 10
PRAYER AND UNEXPECTED BLESSINGS

Prayer was an integral part of our ministry. For many years, before we began our staff work day, we spent an hour in prayer. Our time typically began with a short teaching and then flowed into corporate or private prayer. It was open to our staff as well as anyone who wished to attend.

Through these times, we learned that God answered specific prayer request while preparing us for things He wanted us to hear and do. We learned that prayer is not just telling God the things we need or desire, but more importantly, listening to what He wants to say to us. "However, when He, the Spirit of truth, has come, He will guide you into all truth; for He will not speak on His own authority, but whatever He hears He will speak; and He will tell you things to come" - John 16:13.

One September, after our morning teaching time, I knelt at the left side facing the altar in silent prayer. Suddenly, I heard these words. "When the opportunity comes for you to go to Israel - go." The last thing in the world I was thinking about was going to Israel! But, as I have learned, if something does not make sense now, just put it on a shelf. Don't try to make something happen or try to figure it out. Just put it on a shelf and stay open to God.

About a week later, I received a phone call from a pastor friend, Al Detter. He called to invite me to travel to Israel in November. Through sponsoring many tours, he was able to offer me a total 2-week all-inclusive package at a greatly reduced price. I did not need to pray about it because I had already heard from heaven!

That November, I traveled throughout Israel retracing the footsteps of Jesus. I floated on the Dead sea, sailed on the Sea of Galilee and visited many historic Biblical sites. It was an amazing learning experience for which I am extremely grateful.

I remember visiting Caesarea Philippi where Jesus took his disciples. There, in response to Jesus' inquiry, Peter declared Jesus to be the Christ (Matt 16:13-19). Then, Jesus said "Blessed are you, Simon Bar-Jonah, for flesh and blood has not revealed this to you, but My Father who is in heaven. And I also say to you that you are Peter, and on this rock, I will build My church, and the gates of Hades shall not prevail against it." – Matt 15:17-18.

Jesus was not saying that Peter was the rock. Jesus was saying the truth revealed to Peter, that Jesus is the Christ, that, is the rock upon which the Church is built.

The region where Jesus intentionally took his disciples to declare and reveal this truth was renown as an area of occultic idolatry. The rock outcroppings surrounding this area create a natural amphitheater. Carved in the upper walls were numerous slots where idols had once been displayed. Gushing from the lower regions of this natural feature, springs of water once flowed from which it was believed beings from the underworld proceeded.

It was with great intention that Jesus took his disciples there, to boldly confront the idolatry and religious error of his day and to boldly proclaim he was the Messiah. This area was called "Hells Gates" and Jesus was saying believers never need fear the gates of hell, or the world's culture, because Jesus will build his triumphant church on His Lordship and the knowledge, he reveals to us! That primary knowledge is that Jesus is the Christ! The day of Jesus' resurrection, the waters mysteriously ceased flowing from "Hell's Gates".

Pam was not able to travel with me on this trip in the year 2000. There were other commitments at home, but she was thrilled that I was able to go. We dreamed about a future time when, together, we would be to visit Israel. That time came in 2017.

It began in August of that year while we were attending our annual ministers retreat in Lancaster, Pennsylvania. We had our two oldest grandsons with us and were staying in a hotel. We had been enjoying the indoor pool and I had just left Pam and the boys to take the elevator to our third-floor room. As I stepped off the elevator, suddenly the Spirit of God said, "Pastor Detter is going to call you."

I thought, "That's interesting", as I swiped my key card to enter the room. When I open the door, my phone was ringing. I saw on the caller ID that it was Pastor Detter.

After we exchanged greetings, he said to me. "As you know, Marie and I have hosted many trips to Israel and because of our accumulated credits, we can take two guests with us on our scheduled trip this November."

He went on to tell me, "We made a list of all the potential people we could ask. We have been praying over the list, asking the Lord to show us who to ask. This week we heard from the Lord. He said, 'The persons I want you to ask are not on the list. I want you to ask, Jim and Pam Dumont.'"

It was somewhat strange as he apologized for not having us on the list while at the same time telling us that Jesus had trumped his list and moved us to the front. Again, this was not something we had to spend a lot of time to discern God's will. It was an answer to prayer and the fulfillment of a long-standing dream. That fall, we went to Israel, but not without the devil contesting what God had so graciously planned for us.

On October 23rd, Pam was working in our yard when she slipped and broke her ankle. The news was devastating. She would be in a cast through the end of the year. That included the time of our Israel trip in November!

As I have said previously, Pam has a "Get -er- done" mentality, so we never considered canceling the trip. We certainly did not want to hinder our group, so we decided to trust God and make it happen. We purchased an all-terrain "knee walker scooter" upon which Pam could prop her leg and off we went!

We were moved to the head of lines during our air travel. On the ground throughout Israel, I pushed Pam up hills and, with a cable attached to the back, held on as she smoothly rolled down hills. A young missionary couple from the Philippines whom we befriended graciously assisted us. Pam even rode a cable car to the top of Masada and toured the peak on her scooter.

On this trip, we retraced my previous trip along the Golan Heights and eventually stopped at a restaurant for lunch. Another tour bus preceded us, and the people were winding down their meal as we arrived.

Navigating through the crowded restaurant, I noticed an African American gentleman siting alone. On his head was a ball cap with the words, "U.S. Marines". As I walked by him, I said "Semper Fi", a shortened version of "Semper Fidelis" which is Latin for "Always Faithful", the Marine Corps slogan. As soon as I said it, he whipped around and said, "Were you a Marine!" I said, "No, I was in the U.S. Coast Guard - Semper Paratus. Semper Paratus is Latin for "always ready" which is the Coast Guard motto.

Without flinching, he shot back, "Close enough, sit down!" Well, this was an initiation I could not dismiss. He then began to tell me his story. In 1966 he was drafted and sent to Viet Nam. He told me from the day he landed in Viet Nam, he was scared spitless. He said his eye glasses were always covered with a layer of dirt because he was constantly facing down, hunched in fear as close to the ground as possible. This went on for some time until one day, tired of living in fear, he called out to God in prayer.

He said, "As I cried out to God, I felt as though a steel mesh encircled my entire body. Instantly, I was delivered of fear and I knew I would survive Viet Nam." He said from that day forward, something took hold of him and he accomplished many exploits. He was not bragging on himself as he inferred of his many exploits. Rather, he was bragging on Jesus and how Jesus had delivered him from the spirit of fear!

What a lesson that day of how God wants his children to live in bold confidence despite whatever we face in life. "For God has not given us a spirit of fear, but of power and of love and of a sound mind" - 2 Timothy 1:7. We were grateful that God had opened to us this amazing trip and glad we had learned to walk in faith and to be undeterred when the enemy tried to rob us of the blessing!

Prayer reminds us of the futility of doing things in the flesh.

Matthew Barnett

Chapter 11
AN ARCHITECT MEETS JESUS

One of the greatest joys we had in 38 years of ministry was the opportunity to introduce people to Jesus and then to spiritually establish them in the faith. Nothing is more exciting than to see a person receive the miracle of the New Birth and then to help them become grounded in God's Word. Only Jesus Christ can change a life and bring spiritual freedom. The only cure for racial animosity, pride, prejudice, bitterness, anger and rejection is for people to find forgiveness and their new identity in Christ.

In Acts 20:32, the Apostle Paul declared, "So now, brethren, I commend you to God and to the word of His grace, which is able to build you up and give you an inheritance among all those who are sanctified." Paul knew that building people on the foundation of God's Word would insure they receive their rich and full inheritance in Christ. That inheritance includes everything God provides in this present life as well as what is ours in the life to come.

Second to the privilege of building lives spiritually was the joy and challenge to build a church campus that will be a lasting resource for years to come. With our last church, Erie Christian Fellowship, we spent 30 years progressively going from rented space to purchasing over 12 acres of prime real estate and eventually building over 45,000 sq. feet of ministry space.

During our last building project, we hired an architect to create a comprehensive plan for our entire parcel of land and existing buildings. This was a very wise decision because it forced us to pray and think long term.

Over the years, we visited many churches and sometimes saw the results of failing to plan long term. I remember visiting a church in Ohio where it was obvious the campus had been progressively constructed without a long-term plan. Everything looked piece meal. The structure was long and narrow. It was obvious additions had been made without working from a strategic master plan. We determined to learn from the mistakes of others and to pray and make wiser decisions.

Toward that end, we knew the time had come for us to hire a professional architect. As in any profession, all people practicing are not the same. Some are better than others in their craft and some are easier to work with than others. One lesson we learned over the years is to go where you have favor. Before making any decisions, remember to pray, be patient and trust God to open the right doors.

That's exactly what we did in seeking an architect. Eventually we settled on the firm that designed and built the school opposite of our campus. They were renown for the wise and creative use of floor space. We needed to work with our existing gymnasium, build for our immediate needs and strategically plan for future expansion. That was a tall order to fill.

One of the reasons we chose the firm we did was because they had an excellent reputation and were willing to work with us. We had favor with them. In our communications, they respected our vision and purpose and never even asked that we sign a contract. We worked in mutual respect and honor. It was a unique arrangement of trust. I believe they were happy to be part of a project that would help families and our community at large.

There were some humorous incidents along the way. Joe, the Chief Architect was a Roman Catholic. Having built many schools and public properties, he excelled in the design and utilization of floor space. However, his concept of a church building was tied to his theology as an old school Roman Catholic.

When we talked about our needs, beyond our sanctuary, some of our concerns included space for our school, fellowship and social space plus a bookstore and coffee shop area. Joe's major concern was an area to display caskets at funerals. Once we worked through those issues, the day came for us to view the artist rendering of the building exterior.

Our entire team sat in suspense, awaiting the great unveiling! When the moment arrived and the drape was withdrawn, silence filled the room. Joe had cloaked his amazing floor design in a very bygone looking exterior. No one knew what to say. His theological perspective had shaped his architectural design.

The good news is our team was gracious and Joe did not wear his feelings on his sleeve. We eventually worked through every detail until everyone was on the same page and we got it right! We had worked through the arduous task of integrating an existing building with our current needs and long-term expansion plans.

Because of Joe's theological mindset that one earns God's graces by good deeds, there were many times when Joe would end a planning meeting by throwing in an unexpected extra perk. It might be a service for which we would not be charged or an upgrade we were not expecting. He greatly blessed us. Then he would say something along the lines of, "You know, one has to do everything they can to be certain they make it to heaven." I lost track of how many times he said that, but I made a mental note that I must clarify for Joe God's plan of salvation.

Finally, the day of our last meeting arrived. Our team sat at folded tables towards the front of the sanctuary. Once again, Joe gladly threw in a professional courtesy followed by his regular hopeful and anticipatory statement that this would count towards his earning a place in heaven.

I knew this was my moment of opportunity. I may never again have the chance to share with Joe God's plan of salvation. So, I leaned over and said, "Joe, when this meeting is over, could I have a few moments of your time?" "Absolutely", he replied.

So, when everyone had left the room, I said, "Joe, first, I want to thank you for all the professional courtesies you have shown us. You have blessed us greatly. It has been a privilege working with you and your team." Joe, of course thanked me for our sincere gratitude.

I then said, "Over the course of this project, I've noted you say many times you hoped the benefits you extended to us would accrue towards earning your place in heaven." He said, "That's right". "Joe", I said, "That is very commendable, but have you ever heard of God's plan of salvation?" As I suspected, he had not.

So, I asked permission to share with him the gospel. I explained that years ago, I had been an altar boy but, I had never heard that heaven is a gift. It is not something we earn or deserve but something God offers to us because Jesus paid the terrible price for our sins by shedding his blood on the cross. I told him the Bible says, "For by grace you have been saved through faith, and that not of yourselves; it is the gift of God, not of works, lest anyone should boast"- Ephesians 2:8–9.

When I was done explaining this, I said, "Joe, have you ever heard this before?" In earnest sincerity and somewhat amazed he replied, "Never". I then quoted the familiar passage where Jesus tells Nicodemus, "For God so loved the world that He gave His only begotten Son, that whoever believes in Him should not perish but have everlasting life"- John 3:16.

I then told him what work Jesus said God requires. Jesus once was asked this specific question. His response is recorded in St. John's gospel: *"This is the only work God wants from you: Believe in the one he has sent"* - John 6:29, NLT.

I said, "Joe, would you like to receive the gift of eternal life and know with certainty that your sins are forgiven, and you have a guaranteed home in heaven?" Without hesitation, he immediately replied, "Absolutely!"

So right there, I led Joe in a prayer of salvation. I asked him to repeat this simple prayer after me.

"God in heaven, I come to you now in the Name of your precious Son, Jesus Christ. I acknowledge that I have sinned and I sincerely repent. Thank you for sending Jesus to die in my place. Thank you for raising him from the dead so that I can be forgiven and granted eternal life. I believe Jesus Christ is the Son of God and soon coming King. Amen."

As soon as Joe said, "Amen", he grabbed his chest. It surprised me. I honestly wondered if he was ok. Before I had the chance to inquire, pointing to his chest, Joe said without any prompting, "Something just happened in here!". In amazement, he said it again, "Something just happened in here!" And then I got it. I had never seen such a dramatic and evident demonstration of the impartation of eternal life.

Joe was miraculously born again just like Jesus said in John 3:3. Never again would he ever have to question his eternal destiny. His days of working to earn salvation were over. He had received an impartation of God's gift of eternal life. This is what the Bible calls being "born again". "Having been born again, not of corruptible seed but incorruptible, through the word of God which lives and abides forever" - 1 Peter 1:23 (NKJV).

Joe lived a few more years after this incident and one day he left this earth to transition to heaven. He was a good man who truly cared for people but needed someone to clarify to him the simple but profound gospel. There are many people like Joe, who spend their lifetime uncertain of their destiny because no one has taken the time to explain to them the simple plan of salvation. At Joe's funeral, I rejoiced with his wife and adult children. No one questioned where Joe was.

Dear reader, how about you? Are you still doing your best to earn God's graces in your life? Remember, Jesus said the only work God requires is that we acknowledge our need (repent) and receive His Son, Jesus. Jesus alone has the power to forgive your sin and impart God's gift of eternal life. Why not, right now, pray the same short prayer I prayed with Joe? God is no respecter of persons. What he did for Joe, he will do for you if, like Joe, you come to him in sincere faith.

"God in heaven, I come to you now in the Name of your precious Son, Jesus Christ. I acknowledge that I have sinned and I sincerely repent. Thank you for sending Jesus to die in my place. Thank you for raising him from the dead so that I can be forgiven and granted eternal life. I believe Jesus Christ is the Son of God and soon coming King. Amen."

Satan laughs at our toiling, mocks at our wisdom
and trembles when we pray.

Unknown

Chapter 12
DELIVERANCE AND NEW DESTINY

In all our years of ministry, I recall one of the strangest days was the day
we were called upon to minister deliverance to a young lady oppressed
by demons. This was not the first time we were involved in such
ministry. In fact, twice before, a close friend who pastored a very large
Baptist church in our community had asked me and another Spirit filled
pastor to help in delivering someone oppressed by demons. In both
incidents, the person needing help was recommended by a psychologist
who understood the problem extended beyond the scope of medical
science.

It should not seem strange that such ministry is needed today. In Mark
16:17, Jesus said, "And these signs shall follow them that believe; In my
name shall they cast out devils; they shall speak with new tongues."
Never did we go looking for devils or demons, however, when the need
arose or they manifested or challenged our authority in Christ, we
would never retreat.

This day, I received an unexpected phone call. Would I come and pray
for a young woman who was manifesting strange demonic
manifestations? She would slip into a trance like state and then with
eyes rolled back, she would utter demon like gibberish. This was not in
any way like the pure, heavenly prayer language one receives when
baptized in the Holy Spirit. This was clearly oppressive, controlling and
demonic.

Today, many people in the industrialized world do not acknowledge or understand demonic activity. More and more pop stars and music icons acknowledge the dark and hidden world through symbols and lyrics while many in the church and intellectual community refuse to acknowledge anything supernatural. People, it seems, fall into a ditch on either side of the road. Either they categorically deny anything supernatural or they focus on the devil to the point of paranoia and fear.

By his example, Jesus set the correct balance in dealing with demonic activity. He did not seek demonic encounters but, when demons challenged his ministry or when someone's healing or spiritual freedom required deliverance, Jesus exercised his authority and faced demons head on. We always sought to follow that same guideline.

When our office received the call, we were told that there had been some dabbling in occult activity by the girl needing deliverance. Always there is some "open door" that has given the devil a legal right to get his foot in the door. The people who called were driving with the girl in a car and were not far from a country community church where we were friends with the pastor.

We called the church and were given permission to use their building to meet with the girl and the people with her. I then contacted my associate, Pastor Jason and said, "Let's go".

When we arrived, the girl was sitting in a car in the church parking lot. She was in the back seat in a zombie like state muttering strange gibberish. Eventually she was directed out of the car and into the church where we could minister to her.

It is important for every believer to know the power of Jesus' blood and how thoroughly Jesus defeated Satan on the cross. Scripture declares in Colossians 2:15 (NCV) "God stripped the spiritual rulers and powers of their authority. With the cross, he won the victory and showed the world that they were powerless."

Before engaging in any spiritual battle, it is critical to know that victory has already been won through Jesus Christ. We always engage the enemy from the vantage point of Jesus' victory. Therefore, we never allow Satan to control the encounter or to have the upper hand.

We immediately took authority in Jesus' name and broke Satan's control over the young lady. Through her lips, the enemy would contest, but we were relentless in standing our ground until she experienced freedom.

I eventually led her in a prayer and declaration to renounce Satan and any doors she had opened to his influence in her life. Eventually she was set free and filled with God's Holy Spirit. It was beautiful to see the transformation in her life.

As we finished our time and were leaving, some of the young people who had come asked if we would visit a home in Erie where they had dabbled in occult practices. Would we pray over the home for cleansing and protection? I agreed to go.

When I showed up at the house, I had no idea of what would unfold. Apparently, there was an unresolved custody situation at the home. As I waited outside, a lady whom I had never met approached and while glaring at me, chillingly declared, "I don't like you!" I knew her problem was not with me, but rather with Jesus in me.

As I patiently waited and assessed the situation, things began to escalate. Someone called social workers to mediate the apparent custody situation. The woman who didn't like me, ended up near the sidewalk speaking with the social workers. She became more and more agitated, working herself into a frenzy until the police were called. By the time the police arrived, the woman was laying on the ground in hysteria.

At this point, I was standing off to the side observing with the social workers. The police were not sure what to do with the woman, so I walked over to pray for her. As I stepped by the woman's side, she curled up like a viper, hissed and lunged at me. Amazed and perplexed, the police asked me to please step aside as they called an ambulance.

As I said, we never look for a demonic encounter, but this day it seemed like everywhere I went I encountered demonic activity. As I stepped back to where the social workers were gathered, with saucer like eyes they astonishingly asked me, "What did we just see!" I said, "Ladies, you just saw your first demons."

Eventually the ambulance arrived, and the woman was taken away. Along with the ambulance came a fire truck. By the time the afternoon was over, the neighborhood had been filled with police, social workers, firemen, and EMT workers. I could not help but think that this is what the Apostle Paul experienced many times as he pushed into unreached areas to spread the gospel message.

At times, when we move into Satan's unchallenged arenas, things get stirred up like a hornet's nest. That is why we should always embrace God's promise, "Now thanks be to God who always leads us in triumph in Christ, and through us diffuses the fragrance of His knowledge in every place"- 2 Corinthians 2:14 (NKJV).

A couple of very interesting things came about as a result of the day's activities. One is funny and the second is a testimony to God's goodness and grace.

The first concerns Jason, my associate's (and now Senior Pastor) response to the first deliverance session with the girl. He had never experienced anything like this. Jason humorously said that I should never again be allowed to take a vacation or be away from the church. He did not want to be left alone should we receive another such call. The good news is that having gained knowledge and experience, I am certain Pastor Jason is now ready for such a task.

The second interesting upshot of the event concerns a young man who showed up as we were leaving the church after the first girl's deliverance. Never had I seen this young man, but he impressed me as being quite strange.

He talked a ghetto type lingo in a high pitch voice and challenged me on my theology. I thought, "Who in the world is this strange man?" Frankly, I did not have time to mess with him, but I thought, "I hope I never see him again." He was just an irritation.

A few weeks later he showed up at our church! He came for a few weeks and then disappeared for about six months. The day he reappeared, he caught up with me in the foyer and politely asked if he could briefly speak with me. I thought, "Here we go."

To my surprise, he said the Lord had told him to come and sit and be quiet and listen. In the back of my mind, I said to myself, "Well, the Lord hasn't told me anything. We'll see how this works out."

Well, years passed, and he and his family are still at ECF church. His children have attended our Christian school, Leadership Christian Academy. I learned some of his background. He's uncertain of his family of origin and grew up in a strange kind of "hyper" religious environment. Not being sure of his family and with poor examples of the faith, he naturally acted out. That was the nature of the young man I initially encountered. He was struggling for identity and a father's love.

But he did hear from heaven and did obey God's directive to humble himself, and to sit and listen. As a result, God brought many people into his life to mentor, gently guide and to instruct him. Today, I call him a friend and am still amazed at how Jesus continues to work through us to seek and save the lost. "The LORD is merciful and gracious, Slow to anger, and abounding in mercy"- Psalm 103:8.

> Peter was therefore kept in prison, but constant prayer was offered to God for him by the church.
> Acts 12:5

Chapter 13
A PRAYING CHURCH
AS TOLD BY PAM

Some things come out of left field and then there are other things that come from a completely different ball park. On September 24, 2018, we faced the greatest challenge of our lives. This ball came from another realm.

When we arrived in Erie Pennsylvania so many years ago, we came to plant a flag; a flag of dedication and commitment to the Lord and to God's call upon our lives. This would be the assigned mission field for two fresh faced servants of God from Maine. We were honored to have an assignment of any kind! Erie, Pennsylvania turned out to be a lovely place to raise a family and plant a church.

The decision to obey God's directive concerning our assignment was not made lightly and, we were determined to remain where we were planted. We fully expected to Pastor in Erie the remainder of our lives.

We learned later that Pastors often are called to both a community as well as to a specific church. Also, long-term pastors produce a special kind of fruit: a fruit of legacy and honor. The rapid rate at which some churches rotate their pastors never allows the fruit of ministry to develop, mature and reproduce. Young trees may produce a measure of fruit, but the overwhelming harvest comes from trees with roots that have grown deep and strong by weathered many seasons.

As we continued to serve the Lord, the ministry years passed, and this assignment was indeed the greatest honor of our lives. Jesus doesn't want us to do ministry for him but rather with him. The same inner witness that directed us to Erie, continued to guide and direct us throughout each season.

Though we determined to be faithful Pastors and leaders of Erie Christian Fellowship Church, we began to sense that our long tenure of pastoring was ending, and a new season was on the horizon. The church's best interest was always in the forefront of our thinking and we recognized the season to pass the baton was nearing.

Capable leadership had been raised up. We knew our time at the helm was coming to an end and we went to Maine to rest before we made a church wide announcement. Decisions made by the direction of the Lord are always easier to make and the peace of His Presence helps us carry them out.

John 10:27 in the Amplified version says, "My sheep know and are listening to my voice and I know them, and they follow me." In a day when many voices are screaming for attention across many platforms, the still small voice of the Lord often is drowned in the chaos. It is His voice that imparts direction, clarity and peace.

One of the defining marks of the disciple is the desire and discipline to be purposeful setting time aside to sit quietly in His presence. During these times, the Word becomes alive, clarity is given, prayers become effective and Jesus is honored.

How can one ever know the sweet voice of the Lord without taking time to listen? Hearing the still small voice of the Lord is a natural outcome of a life wholly devoted to God. This is God's design and it is His idea! Yet, this is one of the disciplines so easily overlooked because it requires one to be reverent and quiet. Learning to hear the voice of God can be the difference between life and death as we soon found out.

Very early that day, when we arrived in Maine, we had no idea just how much the practice of listening to His voice would bring life out of death.

All the way to Maine, Jim and I had talked about the future God held in store for us. Almost 40 years prior, we had traveled this same highway as we headed toward Oklahoma to begin our journey of faith.

September 24, 2018 was a beautiful fall day in Maine. I had cooked dinner while Jim rested from the long drive from Pennsylvania. When he arose, he asked how long dinner was going to be and I replied, "Oh, in about 20 to 30 minutes." Seeing it was such a lovely day, he decided to take a brief stroll outside while I wrapped up the last portion of our evening meal.

Normally, he would stroll to his parent's breath-taking back yard and sit on the dock. Today, he decided to walk along the road and go down to the public boat launch. That small choice would be one of many amazing things that would be part of a great miracle.

Jim's health and fitness has never been a topic of concern for us. He had trained with the Navy SEALS in their diving school and he had lived a life of great physical discipline, exercise and good eating habits. His brief walk outside was of no concern for me.

As I stirred the soup, something started stirring in my heart. I had a growing sense that something was terribly wrong. I have endeavored to listen intently for any instructions the Lord gives me. Although I did not hear a voice, the sense that something was dreadfully wrong continued growing with intensity. Within a minute, I knew I had to go.

There was only one problem. For the past few years, Jim's beautiful mother had been slipping into the long goodbye that Alzheimer's and Dementia cruelly brings to suffers. In times past, she was a fantastic cook and so she wanted to help whenever the pots and pans came out. We

had to protect the food from her "assistance" and protect her from the hot stove.

She was known to set hot mitts on fire and add the most creative additions to our meals. I had prepared a meal previously and turned my back and she helped me by putting a box of donuts into my steam carrots. After a good rinsing, they became the sweetest carrots we had ever eaten!

With a growing sense of "danger" rising within me, I knew I had to go. I said to the Lord, "If she ruins the meal, she ruins it, but please protect her from the heat." In haste, I turned everything off, took the knobs off the stove and hid whatever I could. Both my father and mother in law were at the front door and were puzzled as to why I was so intent to leave.

Forcing my way past my mother in law who did not want me to leave, out the door I went! I felt terrible for being so firm with her, but I had to go. Not knowing why or what I would find, I rushed out the door as fast as I could. When I got to the end of the driveway, I looked down the hill by the boat launch and it was then that I saw two ambulances and a police car.

At first, I felt somewhat relieved because I thought that Jim must be praying for somebody. Jim would always pray for people who were in accidents or in trouble. I thought someone must have had a boating accident and Jim is praying for that man. My heart was filled with compassion as I prayed for this person who was unknown to me.

At first, I didn't think it was Jim because the man had a great big pot belly and Jim is slender and trim. As I drew closer, I recognized his pants and, to my horror, it was Jim. My heart went from being filled with compassion to shock. This man was not unknown to me; this was my beloved husband! At that moment, my world came crashing down. I was in shock and I couldn't believe what I was seeing. My world fell apart.

A team of EMT's were diligently doing CPR and during the extended CPR process air had filled Jim's stomach creating the potbelly. I cried out,

"That's my husband" as a policeman pulled me away from the scene. All I wanted was to be near him, hold him, pray and comfort the man I loved.

I have never been resistant to a police officer, but this young policeman had to hold me back. He was both a comfort and an obstacle in my life. At one moment, I held onto him and the next moment I tried to run from him. I thanked him later for not arresting me for resisting an officer. The young policeman had the difficult task of getting information about the stranger on the street and helping the woman who loved this man.

Three complete strangers had come to Jim's rescue and started CPR. A young mother named Amanda found him, face down, in the middle of the road. She parked her car in the road so no one would hit him. With the help of a good Samaritan, Sandy, they rolled Jim over. They described him as, "Purple and it wasn't looking good." The third good Samaritan, Scott had learned CPR 20 years prior. He knelt and started doing CPR on Jim while they waited for an Ambulance to arrive.

When I arrived, the paramedics were working diligently and with great precision. They took a testing break for a moment to see if Jim was breathing. At this point, they removed the mask and I saw my husband's purple face and eyes. His eyes were red and yellow and fixed like glass. He was gone.

I could not understand why they were still at the scene and not rushing off and then I thought after seeing Jim's eyes, "They don't rush off for a dead man". My mind and heart felt such anguish. There are no words to describe how awful this was. I have never felt so helpless, vulnerable and alone in my life. I did the only thing that I could. I called an elder in our church to pray.

The Bible gives many instructions concerning prayer and the different types of prayer. One kind of prayer is to call for the elders of the church. Right there on the road, with my cellphone, I called our longtime friend and elder, Paul Luciano. At this point, we weren't sure what happened to Jim. Everyone on the scene thought he had been hit by a car. All we knew is he had no pulse.

The spirit of faith rose up in Paul and came through the phone with power. Paul immediately declared, "Pam, according to Psalm 118:17, Jim shall not die but live and declare the works of the Lord!" That Word of the Lord deposited faith into my heart and immediately became, "peace be still" words for me.

We all need one another. Paul's words and his great spirit of faith gave me strength and it also moved our church into an Acts 12:5 kind of action - "Peter was therefore kept in prison, but constant prayer was offered to God for him by the church".

Within a few minutes, 700 miles back in Pennsylvania, a prayer meeting was called at Erie Christian Fellowship Church. People stopped what they were doing. They left their dinners on the table and within an hour one hundred people had gathered to pray for their Pastor.

Like Peter, great prayer was made unto God on Jim's behalf. Our friends and church family would not be denied the life of their Pastor. Never underestimate the power of a group of people praying the prayer of faith in agreement. Strong faith in the Name of Jesus will save the sick and tap into God's miracle working power (James 5:15).

It was their prayers that carried both of us during those same three hours that I thought Jim was gone. Those prayers carried Jim from death's door and carried me into God's presence.

Pastor Jason Ackerman leading Erie Christian Fellowship in prayer
for Pastor Jim – Sept 24, 2018

I shall not die, but live, and declare the works of the LORD. – Psalm 118:17

Chapter 14
AT DEATH'S DOOR
AS TOLD BY PAM

I have walked with Jesus my entire life. I grew up going to church. My parents and two sisters lived on Air Force Bases all over the world and, regardless of our location, I remember being in church three times every week.

When I was about five, I had a growing awareness of Jesus' presence. His great love became real and very precious to me. I was a quiet, freckle faced, pigtailed little girl whose military family moved often. I learned that no matter where I moved, my best friend, Jesus was already there! The constant loss of friends at the end of every school year as families were transferred caused my relationship with Jesus to deepen. He was always there!

The depth of His majesty and glory never occurred to me as I talked to, "my best Friend". I had no idea that Jesus was the King of Kings and the Lord of Lords. I just knew Him as the "best buddy" I ever had. Jesus was my constant companion and I always sensed His presence. I would talk to him about all the things that were important to a little girl. I would show Jesus my new dress, talk to Him about daisies, seahorses, and tadpoles by the creek bank.

Seeing Jim's lifeless body on the side of the road was the hardest moment of my life. The emptiness of those eyes fixed like glass was like a spear piercing my heart. I knew that he was gone. Never in my entire life have I felt so helpless and vulnerable. I immediately cried out to my dearest friend, Jesus

The best description of my desperation and vulnerability of this moment can compared to a snail's response to danger. The body of the snail is tender and easily crushed. When danger comes, a snail instinctively retreats into it shell and shuts the door!

As I stood by Jim on the side of the road, I immediately crawled into the arms of my very best friend, Jesus, and slammed the door shut! My whole world was crashing down, and I ran to Jesus, my High Tower and Fortress. Proverbs 18:10 says, "The name of the Lord is a strong tower and the righteous run to it and are safe." It was those strong arms that would hold my heart and still my mind in the days to come.

The sudden reality I now faced forebode no good outcome. As my heart, mind and soul were trying to process this, I was also aware I now had the sole responsibility for two sweet elderly people as well as the responsibility for potentially difficult decisions.

In slow motion, as the minutes ticked by, I had a growing concern that my father in law would see this nightmare. I could not let that happen. I kept one eye on Jim and one eye on the road. When the EMT's finally lifted Jim onto a stretcher, I had to make a very difficult decision. I had to leave Jim in the capable hands of the township paramedics so that I could go back to the house and prevent his father from coming to the scene. This was something that no parent or spouse should ever see.

As my concern for Jim's father grew, I said to the policeman, "How on earth am I ever going to walk into his parent's home and tell these two 92-year-old seniors that their 'baby' was found lifeless". He offered to come with me and together we walked towards the house. But, before I left the scene and while still being held by the policeman, I shouted to Jim, "You will live and not die, in Jesus Name!"

Some conversations one never imagines they will have. The walk up the hill and into driveway was the longest walk of my life. I had to willfully place one foot in front of the other. Sure enough, my father in law,

John Dumont Sr. was standing outside the front door anxiously waiting my return. The closer the policeman and I got, the paler his face became.

Jeremy, the Monmouth policeman spoke very kindly to Dad in the kitchen while I kept Jim's mother away from the conversation. As Alzheimer's claimed more and more of Mom's mind, she become childlike. As awful as the disease is, at least she was spared the pain of a mother knowing her child was in critical trouble. Unaware of what we were dealing we, she grabbed my hands as I walked into the house and said, "Let's sing and dance". I could barely move, let alone dance. It was all I could do to maintain my composure. I needed the Lord's strength and wisdom amid this storm.

For the next 3 1/2 hours, the uncertainty of whether Jim was dead or alive would flood my heart and mind. The last thing I saw were those empty eyes staring into space. The policeman forbade me to drive, so I called friends to take us the 15 miles to Central Maine Medical Center in Lewiston. There, I found myself sitting in the waiting room with my sister Elizabeth, Jim's parents, John and Anita and Jim's Aunt and Uncle, Dot and Gerry.

God provided great strength both within and without. As I sat in silence, I clung to my sister and longed to see my beloved. Jim's uncle Gerry took the lead role in speaking to the hospital staff. In life, even the strongest among us need each other. I needed the strength of this special little group. They provided the sweetest and most tender care when I needed them the most.

Eventually, after what seemed like an endless wait, we were soberly informed that we must all go into another room. The collective moan said it all. After longing for any news, what words was I about to hear?

The walk toward that new room was long, and I could barely move. My sister grabbed me by the waist and walked with me into the dreaded conference room. The silence was deafening, and we thought we were going to be told the worst news that any parent or wife could ever hear. Up to that point, everything was in a hurry. Now, I wanted to slow the scene down and, if possible, to delay it.

While we waited for another extended time, two women arrived to pray. Previously, I had met one of the ladies. She was one of my mother in-law's caregivers and had been at a prayer meeting when the news came that Jim was down. She and a friend immediately left the prayer meeting and drove an hour to pray for a man they hardly knew.

When Marie and Louise walked in, their arrival was like two angels visiting the waiting room. They were sent to pray and boldly pray they did! My mind flashed to all the hospital visits we had done over 37 years of pastoring. Being on the receiving end was like heaven coming to earth! Their prayers gave me strength. How does one say thank you for two strangers spending hours with you in prayer? They were a part of this amazing miracle and I will forever be grateful to God for sending them.

<u>The news</u>

Soon, the first of many wonderful doctors came into the room. I could barely breath as my whole life depended on the next few words this doctor would speak. When he told me that Jim was alive, relief flooded my being! Justin and Anna, our son and daughter-in-law (both Medical Doctors) were on speaker phone and the three physicians discussed Jim's case in terms that only they could understand.

We were told that paramedics had revived Jim's heart. The big question was, how long had Jim been down? The longer the brain is without oxygen, the greater the damage.   I was extremely grateful that he was alive and in their great care. Now I faced the next uncertainty, was his brain dead or alive?

Seeing Jim

My heart's desire was to see Jim and when I was finally allowed, I was not prepared to see his condition. He was wired from head to toe with multiple drips going into his veins. He was on a breathing machine and wrapped in a barometric suit to chill his body temperature down to 90 degrees. They put him in a coma to protect his brain until they could figure out what had happened to him.

That first night was the longest night of my life but I found great comfort in the texted photos I received of the 3-hour prayer meeting our church conducted on Jim's behalf. They prayed for my strength as well as for the journey ahead of me. Sleep is something I would not experience for a few days.

I slept only 15 minutes that first night. Cindy, my younger sister, came in the next day and made me lie down. She sat by my side and promised to care for both Jim and me. Words cannot express the love, respect and appreciation I had for her at that moment. Knowing my RN sister was there, I slept for 30 minutes. That was the greatest gift she could have ever given to me.

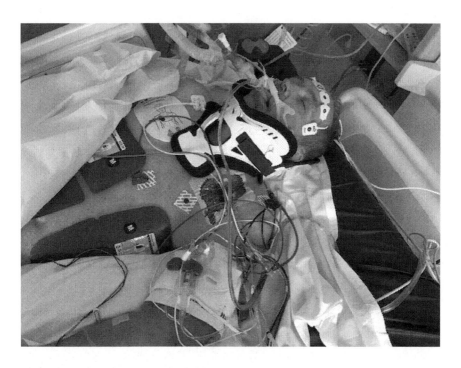

Jim in his six-day coma.

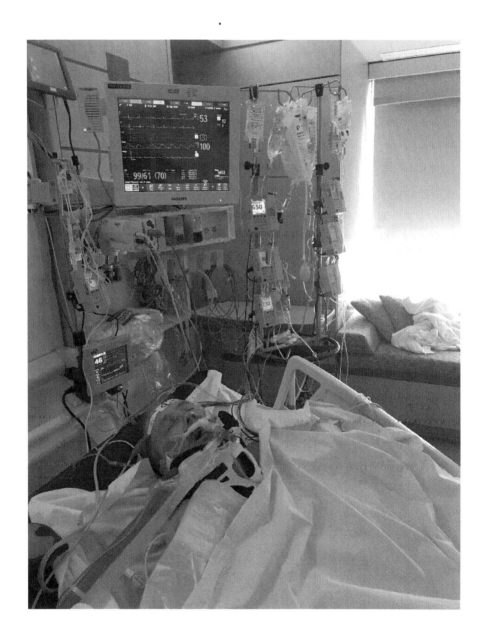

Yea, though I walk through the valley of the shadow of death, I will fear no evil; For You are with me; Your rod and Your staff, they comfort me. - Psalm 23:4

Chapter 15
THE LONG WEEK
AS TOLD BY PAM

Jim was supposed to wake up from his medically induced coma in 36 hours, but he lingered for days. Around the clock, the intensive care medical staff attended to his needs. They checked on him every 2 hours, testing his reflexes for any sign of recovery and neurological change. They would pinch and poke his toes and touch his raw eye balls for any response. Day after day, Jim remained unresponsive and showed no reaction to pain.

Our son Justin and his family arrived from Pittsburgh on Tuesday night. Their arrival was such a comfort. As a Physical Medicine and Rehab Doctor, Justin knew what we were facing. He immediately took over the medical conversations and care program freeing me to be the loving wife. I did what I knew to do, stay close to Jesus.

Over the years, I learned from walking with others in crisis, that prayer is often harder for those personally involved. Those being tossed and turned in the middle of the storm would often express their inability to pray. Now, I knew what they meant.

I would tell our friends. "This is a partnership. Both sides have a part to play. For my part, I'll do the praying and your part is to do the praising." Praise has been called "the highest form of prayer" for it takes our focus off the problem and puts it on the Greater One, our God who is bigger than any problem we face.

Laying before me was the biggest problem and greatest challenge I had ever faced. Jesus didn't need for me to be "a reporter" and tell Him all the issues and problems. He already knew what we were facing.

For many years, I had taught on prayer and led prayer meetings and retreats. I grew to love this precious part of our Christian life. In prayer, our mind has a degree of involvement but in praise, the focus is on God and His Greatness. In His presence, problems are resized, and peace quiets the fears we face.

Now, I was face to face with life and death. The situation before me was dire, options were few and fear threatened to overwhelm me. My mind was frozen, but my spirit was free. I could find no words in my mind to pray, but I could praise from my heart! This was not praising God *for* the situation but praising Him *despite* the situation.

So, I turned on my worship streaming app and curled into the arms of Jesus! There, I stayed for six days. I needed to quietly be in His presence drawing strength while others were doing the praying. Isaiah 26:3 says, "You will keep him in perfect peace, whose mind is stayed on You, because he trusts in You."

The valley of the shadow of death

Doctors were puzzled as to why Jim lingered for days in his medically induced coma. No medical reason or explanation could account for this. For me, it was like walking through "the valley of the shadow of death". Not knowing if my husband was recovering or had departed and was just being maintained by life-support, I stood over him and planted another flag - a flag of faith and of honor.

Long ago, Jim and I had made a critical decision. Considering Jesus' ministry of healing the sick and, in the light of God's many promises, we determined we would rather die, in faith, believing God for healing than to die in doubt and unbelief. Each of us will one day die, and we didn't want to face the Lord and say, "We didn't think You could do it this time".

When I focused on our previous determinations and the ultimate outcome of meeting Jesus face to face, a new resolve took hold of my heart. Fear lost its grip on me.

There were many unknowns in that moment, but my vow to stand in faith was certain. It was a powerful moment, as I stood there and made a declaration of faith. I was going to honor Jesus by standing in faith. Having planted the faith of flag, peace flooded my heart.

I continued the vow by the purposeful determination that by God's grace, I would bring honor to the Lord Jesus in everything that I said and did. By His strength, I wanted to be a great witness for Him. With a boldness that only comes from the authority of Jesus' name, I reminded the Devil that Jim has served God his whole adult life and you are not taking him like this. Jim was born in this hospital, but he isn't going to die here!

As I was standing on the edge of the shadow of death's door, every success we had experienced faded away and every problem now looked small and petty. The successes were never ours to claim. They always belonged to Jesus and, it was Him working through us that brought fruit.

From heaven's perspective, this life looked completely different. There was satisfaction in having lived abandoned to God. Looking at Jim, joy filled my heart because he never quit. I was grateful for the privilege of serving Jesus and incredibly proud of Jim for never quitting the race set before him.

This "flag planting moment" became a turning point for me. I saw no visible change in Jim and the storm still waged, but something had changed in me. My faith was anchored and stabilized in four important ways.

First, by renewing the previous commitment Jim and I had made to stand in faith, God gave me a marked degree of peace that passed all understanding. The situation, in its entirety, was now placed in His capable hands.

Second, taking an eternal perspective made me realize how small are all of life's "big problems". I found myself regretting ever giving these issues a minute of care.

Third, by exercising the Authority of Jesus' Name over any satanic attacks, I got my fight back. Jesus removes every believer from the "victim" seat and wants us to know that all power and authority belong to Him.

And fourth, a deep joy for Jim's faithfulness to the call of God filled me with love and respect for him. I realized that never, throughout eternity, will we ever regret any decision we made for the cause of Christ.

Standing there with one hand raised to God and the other holding the hand of the person I have most loved in this world, a peaceful calm settled over me. Later, the ICU staff said my "temperament in this crisis had a deep impact on them". They knew I was a devout Christian, not because of the words I said, but by my actions and love during this crisis.

From that moment on, whenever we were alone without nurses or visiting family, I closed my eyes and quietly worshipped in the presence of the Lord. There were times, especially in the middle of the night, when the staff would come into the room and I didn't know they were there. They quietly and respectfully worked around me without saying a word.

For 6 days, I remained by Jim's side and in the presence of the Lord. For many years, I have purposed to sit quietly in the Master's presence at the start of every day. I wanted to please the Master, so, I would sit in His presence.

There were times when I would experience profound peace and, other times, I heard specific instructions for that day. This discipline became a constant in my life, and, through it, I learned how to push aside the world and to focus on Him. I never dreamed that all those years of private and personal discipline would be called upon and put into practice in such a way.

Jim was supposed to wake up in 36 hours, but he didn't wake up that day, or the next, or the next as he continued to linger in a coma. There were a couple of moments when he slightly opened his eyes, but those moments were brief and were gone as quickly as they came.

In his room was a white board where the staff would write the goals each day for the current patient. Only one goal, "Squeeze Pam's Hand", ever appeared on that board. Throughout the week, that goal remained unachieved. I noticed how much quieter the staff were becoming. Even our son and daughter in law became quieter.

The 6th day: Brutal truth and then God shows up!

On the sixth day of intensive care, Saturday at 7:30 a.m., one of the ICU Doctors came in and tested Jim yet again. He looked directly at me and said the words no wife would ever want to hear, "Your husband has brain damage". He went on to explain that Jim had failed every neurological test and we must do something different. I wondered what "something different" was going to be. What would happen next was the big question and the answer would astound everyone,

At 10:00 a.m., after hearing that my husband was suffering brain damage, our four precious grandchildren ages 4 to 12 arrived. The

"Power Team" was now on the scene. They had missed a week of school and needed to return to Pittsburgh. They came to say goodbye to their grandfather; perhaps for the last time.

They entered the room, placed their hands on "Poppy", and began to pray. It was hard for them to see their vibrant grandfather like this. Someone has said, "The strongest prayers come from the purest hearts". They prayed and then they began to sing a sweet little song they had created.

They had made up this little song for their youngest brother and they would all sing it to each other. This day, they sang it to their grandfather. As they sang, suddenly, a miracle occurred! The sweet angelic voices of children singing woke Jim from his long slumber and he pushed through the six-day coma. He opened his eyes - fully awake and alive!

It was a miracle before our eyes. Nothing else had penetrated that deep coma. One moment, he was unresponsive, failing every neurological test and then the next, he was alive, awake and wondering, "Where am I?" Jim went from death to life in a matter of minutes.

The technicians and nurses came streaming into the room to say we have never seen anything like this! Doctors were both delighted and dumbfounded by his sudden recovery. There was a measurable sense of awe and wonder from the hospital staff. They named him, "The golden boy of ICU" and later he became known as, "the Miracle Man".

To allow space in ICU for all our grandchildren to be with Jim, I had left and was sitting in the waiting room. Justin, our son came running into the foyer to get me and shouted, "You have got to go back into the room!" I found my husband awake, conscious and wondering where he was. The previous days were like a nightmare from which I could not wake. Now, it was a dream that I never wanted to end. We were witnessing a miracle! My husband was dead and now he was resurrected to full life

Though he was slow to wake from the coma, once awake, he began to make incredible progress. One nurse told me that his rate of recovery for a brain injury in one day was equal to most people's rate of recovery in one week. The doctors had previously warned me that if he did wake up, he may have to spend 90-120 days relearning to sit, walk and talk. They also cautioned me that oxygen deprivation can dramatically change the personality. I might be married to a man that I did not know and, may not even like.

Now, in one miraculous moment, I had my husband back, fully restored and whole with all his cognitive abilities and personality intact. He has no brain damage; his brain is fully functioning, and he has all his skills. He only lost six weeks of memory, but those are weeks no one wants to remember. His personality remained whole and he is now enhanced by profound gratitude. How does one ever say, "thank you" for a life saved and fully restored?

Widow Maker to Way Maker

The depth of this amazing miracle has continued to unfold. Jim's miracle is three miracles in one.

Throughout the coma days, they scanned Jim's heart and eventually ruled out heart disease as the reason for this huge event. After Jim was awake, a heart cauterization could be done. Through it, they determined that Jim experienced a "widow maker" heart arrest.

On the back of his heart, the Lateral Anterior Descending (LAD) artery had collapsed. This is an area where many electrical systems are located, and it caused Jim's heart to immediately stop. He fell to the ground like a rock with a complete heart arrest. It was later determined that there was some blockage present, but the real culprit was a genetic weakness of that artery. The artery collapsed but to the doctor's surprise, it reopened flooding the heart with blood. The flooding of blood protected Jim's heart from damage.

Though he had a "widow maker", he has no heart disease. There also was no explanation as to why it re-opened but it was the first of many

miracles that brought Jim back to a full life. A stint was put in to protect the artery from ever collapsing again.

The survival rate for "widow maker" heart attack or arrest is very small, less than 3%. Surviving a heart arrest to this degree was a miracle in the first place, but he went through the ordeal with no heart damage. This was the first of three miracles in this amazing story.

For Jim to be without oxygen for more than four minutes and have no brain damage is an even greater miracle than to survive a "widow maker". Over 4 minutes without oxygen is bad and the situation grows worse with each passing minute. The brain suffers from permeant damage when deprived of oxygen.

Taking the testimony of everyone involved from the rescuers, EMT's, and my own timeline which started when Jim asked when dinner would be ready, the best estimates of his downtime without a heartbeat and oxygen are from 8-13 minutes. The lack of response in the medical staff when those numbers where discussed spoke volumes to me. From a natural standpoint, there was little hope.

The estimated stay at a rehab center was to be 90-120 days. The rehab doctor shared with us that a patient who had come earlier with the same thing couldn't sit. Jim walked in and out of rehab in 5 days and this miracle has continued to astound everyone involved.

The third miracle became clear in the next few weeks, Jim's personality was not only preserved, it is now greatly enhanced by the gratitude we feel. Gratitude for all that God has done fills our lives. You don't really know how much you love someone until they are gone. Now, each day is a gift and we are living with a profound sense of awe, wonder and gratitude.

As for me, I am now a Hebrews 11:35 woman. "Women received their loved ones back again from death" (NLT). I am now one of those women. I am also reverently aware that, "To whom much is given, much is expected" - Luke 12:48. I've walked with Jesus my whole life. Throughout each season, my knowledge of Jesus has grown and my love for Him has deepened.

I honestly thought I knew Him, but this miracle has blown the lid off my knowledge of Him. Like the disciples who saw Jesus calm the winds and waves, they bowed down in the boat and worshipped Jesus for the first time. They were filled with awe and wonder and exclaimed with deep reverence, "Who are You that the winds and waved obey You?" - Matt 8:27.

I am now in a new season of reverence and many times have asked, "Who are You that the dead will rise at Your command?" I feel like the richest woman on the planet, if not the most grateful one. For the rest of my days, I will tell His story and share the preciousness of His Person.

In my life, there has been four marked seasons of my relationship with Jesus. From my earliest memories of Jesus being my constant companion, He was first, my "Friend". My knowledge of Him grew as I matured, and Jesus became "Savior" in my teens.

When I was filled with the Holy Spirit at age 21, and for the next 20 years, Jesus was Lord to the degree that I yielded to Him. As we raised a family and grew a church, the tasks were many. I loved Him, but busyness often kept me from the intimacy I once knew. I deeply regret the void I allowed my busy life to create.

Jesus remained my Lord until one day, after a particularly meaningful private devotion time, I entered the fourth season of my knowledge of Him - "Master". I wept when I read the story of Jesus asking His disciples only one thing; "Could you not tarry with one hour?" - Matt 26:40. The Christ was asking from His friends for one thing; an hour! For all He had done for them and for all He has done for us, all He asked in return was a friend to be with Him for one hour. Conviction and resolve filled my heart.

Knowing that Jesus is the Great High Priest still making intercession for us, in sincerity I asked Him, "Do you still want a friend who will pray with you?" I meekly told Him that I would be that friend. Thus, began my mornings where I would arise and say, "Master, your servant awaits." For the past 20 years, that has been my morning prayer. Sitting before Him in quiet reverence has grown my prayer life and it has grown me as a person. It was the lessons I learned during the "Master Years" that I relied on during the most difficult week of my life.

Ps 146:11 instructs us to, "Be still and know that I am God." Out of stillness and reverence we become acquainted with Him. Daniel 11:32 (Amp) goes on to say, "Those that know their God will prove themselves strong and shall stand firm and do exploits."

The merging of those scriptures was the guidepost for this season. Out of a sincere desire to please Him and be a friend to Jesus, I began to know Him. I had no idea of the amount of strength those years would deposit   in   me.

Giving thanks always for all things to God the
Father in the name of our Lord Jesus Christ.
Ephesians 5:20

EPILOGUE

So now, you've heard the story of how prayer changed everything for us. It's not just prayer, but prayer to God in the Name of Jesus. The Bible directs us to, "Give thanks always for all things to God the Father in the name of our Lord Jesus Christ" - Ephesians 5:20.

When I began my quest to find God, I had no idea of what or "Who" I would discover. Like many people, my understanding was clouded by "religious tradition". I had zero knowledge of the Bible. Religion was just a discontinued compartment of my life that I had buried and forgotten. I soon discovered that Jesus is much more than an antiquated "religious compartment".

Colossians 3:4 says Jesus IS our life. He alone can recreate your spirit and fill you with God's love and power. He alone can remove the guilt and shame of past sins and give you hope and a future. In Christ, there is no condemnation or fear.

I'm no longer a wandering, wondering college student. Over the years, we've proved out God's promises through application, experience and trials. We've seen lives changed and restored. I've been raised from the dead!

We can say as did Paul the Apostle, ". . . for I know the One in whom I trust, and I am sure that he is able to guard what I have entrusted to him until the day of his return" - 2 Timothy 1:12 (NLT).

My greatest joy, however, is seeing that my grandkids will not grope through their adolescent and young adult years without God. They are being brought up with a knowledge of Christ and His Word. They are our, "Power Team"!

What about you? Have you been reconciled to God through Jesus Christ? Do you have the certainty that all your sins are forgiven? Should you experience a sudden death event such as I did, are prepared to meet God face to face?

My life was spared so that I can complete my God given assignment to tell everyone that heaven and hell are real. You don't have to fear death or hell if you have surrendered to Jesus and received the merits of his life, death and resurrection.

In Revelation 1:17-18 Jesus says, "Do not be afraid; I am the First and the Last. I am He who lives, and was dead, and behold, I am alive forevermore. Amen. And I have the keys of Hades and of Death."

Jesus alone holds the keys that unlock hell's gates and opens the doors to heaven. Right now, God is waiting to welcome you home. If you have not yet prayed this prayer, I challenge you to pray it now from your heart. Don't let fear or procrastination keep you from receiving what God has sacrificially provided for you in Christ!

The Bible says, "That if you confess with your mouth the Lord Jesus and believe in your heart that God has raised Him from the dead, you will be saved. For with the heart one believes unto righteousness, and with the mouth confession is made unto salvation."

Prayer to Receive Jesus and Cleansing from All Sin

"God in heaven, I come to you now in the Name of your precious Son, Jesus Christ. I acknowledge that I have sinned and I sincerely repent. Thank you for sending Jesus to die in my place. Thank you for raising him from the dead so that I can be forgiven and granted eternal life. I believe Jesus Christ is the Son of God and soon coming King. Amen."

Friend, if you have prayed this prayer, tell someone about your decision. The Scripture says, "And they have defeated him (Satan) by the blood of the Lamb and by their testimony. And they did not love their lives so much that they were afraid to die" - Revelation 12:11 (NLT).

To all who believe and receive, Jesus delivers from the fear of death and gives strength, courage and purpose to live this life with boldness and love!

About the Authors

Jim and Pam Dumont are 1980 & 1981 graduates of Rhema Bible College in Tulsa, Oklahoma. Jim is a U.S. Coast Guard veteran and a 1978 graduate of the University of Maine with a BA in Geology. Additionally, he is a 2000 graduate of Trinity International University in Deerfield, Il where he holds a MA degree in Religion.

The Dumont's are proud parents of their son, Dr. Justin D. Dumont and his wife Dr. Anna M. Dumont. They are especially grateful for their four grandchildren, the "Power Team", Jazna, Coleben, Symeon and Kendru.

After planting and pastoring churches in Northwest, PA for 38 years, their new assignment is to strengthen churches and believers through the spoken word and printed page. Jim emphasizes the subjects of faith, healing and the Holy Spirit. Pam loves to teach on prayer and knowing Jesus more intimately.

You may contact the Dumonts by e-mail at FaithComm154@gmail.com or by writing to: Faith Communications, 5900 Sterrettania Rd., Fairview, PA 16415. Their miracle story as told by CBN can be viewed on YouTube under **"Man Dead for 13 Minutes."**

Made in the
USA
Columbia, SC